THE SCIENCE OF PROBLEM-SOLVING

Available in the Cassell Education series:

P. Ainley and M. Corney: *Training for the Future: The Rise and Fall of the Manpower Services Commission*
R. Althouse: *Investigating Science with Young Children*
G. Antonouris and J. Wilson: *Equal Opportunities in Schools*
N. Bennett and A. Cass: *From Special to Ordinary Schools*
M. Bottery: *The Morality of the School*
C. Christofi: *Assessment and Profiling in Science*
G. Claxton: *Being a Teacher*
G. Claxton: *Teaching to Learn*
C. Cullingford (ed.): *The Primary Teacher*
L.B. Curzon: *Teaching in Further Education* (4th edition)
L. Gibson: *Through Children's Eyes: Literacy Learning in the Early Years*
B. Goacher *et al.*: *Policy and Provision for Special Educational Needs*
H. Gray (ed.): *Management Consultancy in Schools*
L. Hall: *Poetry for Life*
J. Nias, G. Southworth and R. Yeomans: *Staff Relationships in the Primary School*
A. Pollard: *The Social World of the Primary School*
J. Sayer and V. Williams (eds): *Schools and External Relations*
R. Straughan: *Beliefs, Behaviour and Education*
H. Thomas: *Education Costs and Performance*
S. Wolfendale (ed.): *Parental Involvement*

The Science of Problem-solving

A Practical Guide for Science Teachers

Mike Watts

CASSELL

HEINEMANN
Portsmouth, NH

Published in Great Britain by
Cassell Educational Limited
Villiers House
41/47 Strand
London WC2N 5JE

Published in the United States of America by
Heinemann Educational Books, Inc.
361 Hanover Street
Portsmouth, NH 03801

© Cassell Educational Limited 1991

First published 1991

British Library Cataloguing in Publication Data
Watts, Mike
    The science of problem-solving. – (Education)
    1. Great Britain.   Secondary schools.   Curriculum subjects:
    Problem solving
    I. Title
    001.42

ISBN 0–304–31988–0 (Cassell hardback)
      0–304–31985–6 (Cassell paperback)
      0–435–08314–7 (Heinemann Educational paperback)

Typeset by Colset Private Limited

Printed and bound in Great Britain by
Biddles Ltd, Guildford and King's Lynn

Contents

Preface   vii

1 Problems, Problems . . .   1

2 Skills, Processes and Methods of Problem-Solving   26

3 Co-operative Learning, Constructivism and Some
   Implications for Group Work   51

4 Transferring Learning, Owning the Problems   73

5 Classroom Management and Changing the
   Curriculum for Problem-Solving   95

6 Assessment, INSET and Research   117

Appendix 1   139

Appendix 2   144

References   148

Index   156

Dedicated to Sian, Rhian—and Nana

Preface

It might seem a little contradictory to have a book about problem-solving. One main aim of problem-solving, surely, is to learn from doing, not from reading how to do it. Well, perhaps yes and no. There is always a need to develop the arguments for and against, catch up on new ideas and variations, and pick up some background information and useful details — even at the moment when practical problem-solving is successfully underway. A second aim of problem-solving is to highlight the multiplicity of approaches to a solution — and researching ideas from books is certainly one of those.

This book is aimed at classroom teachers and aims to be both a practical guide and a background reader. The balance is important: not so much a practical guide that it reads like a DIY manual; but not so much a reader that it leaves out some nuts-and-bolts detail. Problem-solving in the classroom should not result in making more problems for the teacher. Its virtues should be the delight which youngsters bring to it and the skills they take away — without causing problems in classroom management or supervision.

Perhaps the title should have been 'The Art of Solution-Finding' — it has a happier ring about it somehow. 'Problem' has a sad touch ('problem child'; 'problem parents'; 'Doctor, I've a problem with my bunion . . .' and so on). When we say we are 'problem-solving' it raises the notion that life is dour and full of awkward difficulties — all of which need remedies. As the old adage would have it, 'Life is full of minor and major problems; some days you get both.'

But the title was chosen carefully. While life can have its share of pitfalls, this book is not full of recipes for coping with all possible contingencies. On the whole it concerns aspects of science and technology, of teaching and learning, of skills and processes, of concepts and attitudes, of teachers and students in schools — together in a mixture to be stirred but not shaken. While the book is about schools, science and technology this does not mean the problems discussed have nothing at all to do with real life. Problem-solving in schools is an attempt to make education relevant and applicable — but more of that later.

And — still on the point — there almost certainly is an art to finding solutions. This book, though, focuses instead on the science of the process. There have been numerous attempts to sort out what a 'problem-solving method' might be, and these are discussed in some detail. While there may not be one absolutely definitive method, there are some well-tried and tested routines which are worth considering.

The book is intended for teachers in middle, secondary and upper schools, and is aimed at classroom practitioners of all kinds who want to know more about problem-solving as a strategy for teaching and learning. The focus of the book is problem-solving within science and technology, although the definition of those two terms is deliberately very wide and vague, and encompasses a range of subject concerns.

Chapter 1 draws a picture of problem-solving. In it, the language of problem-solving is explored, a few definitions are framed, some background to problem-solving is examined and an attempt is made to justify the inclusion of problem-solving in every child's curriculum. The next four chapters focus on a series of major questions. Chapter 2, for instance, considers the skills, processes and methods involved in problem-solving. What are the skills, and which are the particular processes involved? How are they learned, and how can we teach so that they can be practised? Can these skills be transferred from problem to problem, and from one context to another?

Chapter 3 looks at the factors which affect learning in individuals and groups as they solve problems. Youngsters are seldom asked to solve problems on their own; they usually work as a team. They are often grouped together to undertake investigations and projects, and have to work co-operatively to arrive at a solution. To what extent does progress depend upon the roles that individuals play? How does the learning environment count? How do we prepare for the negotiation of ground rules? Can we manage the direct teaching of group learning skills?

Problem-solving relies upon the transfer of learning. It is often experiential learning that is brought to bear upon a novel situation or activity. Group problem-solving requires the negotiation of individuals' 'world knowledge', or personal experience, to solve a common task. Such negotiation entails the scrutiny of individuals' personal understandings for validity, coherence and relevance. To what extent can personal ownership be maintained in the face of group scrutiny? Can the 'act of contributing' and the resultant process of negotiations be taught? How are group selections made between several valid contributions? Can models of the 'status of knowledge' be discerned in group work, and is it possible to counsel for the implications of the affective aspects of ownership?

Chapter 4 looks at what it means for learners to 'own' their learning. Problem-solving is often said to make learners more self-reliant, so that they can take charge of the task and make their own decisions as it progresses. If it is possible to 'own' learning, are there different models of ownership of learning within classrooms? Can there be such a thing as 'strong' or 'weak' ownership?

Chapter 5 considers ways in which problem-solving can be managed within the curriculum. It seems like an awful lot of hard work, it can be noisy and seem unruly — is it all worth the effort? This certainly affects those who are beginning the task of moving towards a problem-solving approach in their schools, and part of the chapter considers this move and its implications.

Finally, Chapter 6 considers some of the bulk of research to be found in the area. This chapter is not intended solely for the *aficionado*, but hopefully draws out summaries and implications for the general reader too. It may seem a little odd to leave all the theory until the end, but it is there for those readers who want to delve deeper into the whys and wherefores of problem-solving. That said, there are theoretical bits in parts of the other chapters. Not so much, hopefully, that it gets in the way, but enough to show where some of the ideas come from.

Writing this book has provided a solution to some of my own problems. My interest and concern for problem-solving stretches back some good few years. I am grateful to problem-solvers worldwide for their ideas, problems, methods and solutions. I am indebted to all those colleagues who have helped rein in this particular hobby-horse without too much wearied impatience, have given me food for thought and have allowed me access to their activities in schools and institutions. A central strategy in problem-solving is to 'ask a friend' and I am fortunate to have had many who listened and responded. I hope they are not too unhappy with my interpretation of their support.

I am particularly indebted to Alan West, of the CREST Award Scheme, for his immense appetite problem-solving, his ideas, drive, support and good business. His energy, enthusiasm and personal friendship have fostered this book. In the past I have had invaluable help from the 'old problem-solvers' of the SSCR — John Heaney, Mick Nott, Andy Howlett and Phil Munson. Between them, my colleagues at Roehampton Institute have contrived to give me problems; Di Bentley has helped me solve most of the ones I didn't know I had.

Chapter 1

Problems, Problems . . .

INTRODUCTION

This book is about problem-solving in school science. My 'mind's eye' audience is teachers of science and technology in and around British schools, plagued by all the joys and jeopardies that implies. The expression 'teachers of science' is meant to cover teachers across all ages and phases, and includes any and all who find themselves teaching science in classrooms.

The intention is to provide a book that is more than just a ready fund of problems with recipes for how they might be solved and handy hints for teachers. All these ingredients are here, but not alone: they are each the basis for some fairly wide-ranging discussion. There are books available which simply supply pages of 'ready-to-use' problems and which no doubt serve a valuable need — some of these are mentioned and appear in the references. Such books, though, rather assume a particular kind of problem and particular problem-solving processes, as well as particular views of schools and school science. While this book, too, is based on particular views, my intention is to spell these out a little and not simply leave underlying principles as unspoken assumptions.

There has always been a sense that problem-solving is seen to be a 'good thing', and must be included in school syllabuses just because of that. This rather begs the question: 'What is so good about problem-solving?' Here, in this first chapter, some attempt is made to tackle that issue. The book seeks answers to other questions, too, such as:

'Why should I (a busy teacher of science) do problem-solving?'
'How does it fit with the requirements of the National Curriculum?'
'Does problem-solving actually teach any *science*?'
'What are the best ways to manage it?'
'Does it benefit some youngsters more than others (and, if so, which)?'

The book, then, is not just a treatise on the nature of problem-solving but seeks a rationale for its use in schools. But first, some tasters.

TASTERS?

One assumption underlying the contents of the book is that while science is quite a special kind of activity, it is also part of everyday life. Being scientific is part of being human and acting both in and on life itself. Therefore scientific and technological problems are all around us. For instance:

> An upright freezer at home is part of a cabinet fridge-freezer combination. The freezer door is opened to take something out and then closed again. At the point of closing the door, a gentle hiss is heard and for about the next three or four seconds the door is very difficult to re-open. After that point it opens quite easily.

Why? What is happening in the freezer to prevent the door opening? Has it something to do with the warm air that displaces the cold air that 'falls out' at the bottom of the freezer when the door is opened, and which then rapidly cools down? Or is it a property of the seal around the door. Or is it something else? I read somewhere that the air does not have enough time to cool down to make the seal so instantaneously tight. Is the effect just an annoyance or is there some purpose behind it? Is it possible to turn the effect to advantage in some way?

Perhaps it is not a problem for all. Maybe, though, one or two readers are now finding their place in the text again having been out to listen intently while pushing and pulling at their freezer door.

Then again:

> I have a plastic shower curtain held by a rail across the entrance to the shower. When I take a hot shower, the bottom of the curtain insists on billowing inwards and, usually, sticking perversely to a wet leg.

Why? A first thought would suggest that the combination of water and steam inside the shower ought to cause the curtain to billow outwards. Is the inward draught caused by the rapid convection of the air up through the shower? Or is it an effect of the stream of water from the shower head? Again, can any use be made of this? Is there some way of putting the effect to profitable purpose? (One solution: ignore the problem and install a shower cabinet with glass doors.)

More:

> A very tall skyscraper office block in London (belonging to one of the five clearing banks) sways perceptibly in the wind—as do all tall towers. Like other buildings of its sort it has kitchens, toilets, sinks and fire sprinkler systems on all its many floors and so needs a large tank of water (about the size of a reasonable swimming pool) at the top, which feeds water to all the parts of the system. But if all that water started to slosh around in the tank when the building sways, particularly if it hit the right frequency in a gusting wind and began to build up momentum, there could be real disaster.

What can be done? What should the architects do? Can the designers make use of this phenomenon? I believe that the answer was to install a series of baffles in the tank to help dissipate some of the energy.

These are not problems I have invented but ones that have been around for a while and which find their way into the pages of science journals. And there are many others in everyday life, as Foster (1989) indicates in an article on 'street-wise' physics. Around the home, for instance, there are usually technological problems associated with putting in central heating, fixing the car or growing champion marrows.

Problems come in all shapes and sizes, and from all areas of life — not just school physics. They may be problems, or puzzles that need an explanation, or simply 'itches' that may be the first steps in an investigation to be followed by a few well-thought-out tests to reach an answer. Or, in some cases, there are solutions which seem to be waiting for a problem to happen. However, once one has become caught up in sorting through some of the issues concerned, begun to construct some idea or model of what is going on, pottered through some probabilities and possibilities, started to put up ideas of how some of the more playful thoughts could be eliminated and settled on a couple of likely lines of action to be tested — then that is problem-solving.

My concern, however, is primarily with problem-solving in school science and technology and so almost all of the examples will be drawn from that sort of arena. The skills and processes may be applicable to everyday problem-solving — indeed, they ought to be — but they will be couched in terms of the skills and processes known and understood by science teachers up and down the country.

THREE ASSUMPTIONS

It will become obvious (if it is not already) that this is not a book which is neutral about problem-solving: it *is* seen as a 'good thing', and one intention is to provide an entrée for teachers who want to try it. It is not, though, uncritical and some attempt is made to explore some of the issues in depth.

To begin, I note three main assumptions — all about learning — which underpin the text and to which I return at various times in the ensuing chapters:

- learning is active, not passive
- learning is about ownership of skills
- learning is for life.

While perhaps too many can remember dull and boring lessons in school, the central theme here is that effective learning is active learning. It is a theme explored elsewhere (for example, Beswick, 1987; Dobson, 1987; Baldwin and Williams, 1988; Bentley and Watts, 1989). In general terms, learning is most vibrant and meaningful when the learner is involved — i.e. when the tasks are interactive and learners are fully engaged in the process. Active learning is when the learner takes responsibility for what he or she wants to learn — making decisions about the 'what' and the 'how'.

Hence, learning is not just what happens with books and teachers and schools but continues as we construe everything around us as we work, rest, play and — in particular — solve problems. The case here is that problem-solving *is* active learning, in that the learner must take some responsibility for the problem before he or she can reach a solution; problem-solving involves a set of skills which, through engaging in the exercise, become part of the learner's repertoire and so can be called on again and again. The important point is that problem-solving involves skills, knowledge and understanding that the learner already possesses, and through the act of problem-solving can add new skills to the learner's store. Moreover, these skills and knowledge can transfer from one problem to the next, both in school and out.

And there is the nub. Arguably, education is intended to equip the next adult generation with the knowledge and skills to allow them maximum personal and social growth within life after school; that is, to learn in school things that can be successfully transferred to other contexts. It is an indictment of much schooling that individuals often cannot make these transfers, and learning becomes so contextualized that it remains 'school-book stuff' and almost entirely useless. Notions of ownership and transfer are dealt with more fully in Chapter 4.

The book is premised on a constructivist theory of learning. Constructivism is a growing 'ism' within science education (and elsewhere) and underpins much of what is said here. The issue of constructivism and school science has been widely discussed elsewhere, but the interaction of constructivism with problem-solving is relatively unexplored. Chapter 3 entails discussion of these terms more fully. In that vein, one more example:

> I sit chatting with friends about (of all things) plastic cash cards. Bank cash cards allow the use of a range of services from the self-service cash tills built into high-street bank exteriors. It becomes obvious in the conversation that few in the circle have a clear idea of how the system works, in particular the amount of data actually stored on the card. Or, put another way, it becomes clear that people in the room all have very different ideas about what is happening. For instance, how does the machine know an individual's cash limit for the week and how much cash has been withdrawn from the account so far that week? Since the machine in the wall is simply a terminal, are those data held in the central computer along with the main details of your account, or are they encoded on the card? Requests for cash beyond the limit are rejected instantly—much more quickly, it seems, than if the terminal had to interrogate the main computer elsewhere about the account (compared, say, with the time taken to arrive at one's balance of account).

What is the problem? The problem is one of conceptualizing, in lay terms, something that is common fare for most people: the operation of plastic cash cards. We know of their operation only (usually) through our interactions with them and the systems they tap into.

Do the terminals write on to the card as well as read off it? Just how fast is computerized transfer of information? Normally, we do not need to understand, we simply use the machines. However, a problem occurs when we want to interact with the system in a more meaningful way (when it swallows our card without reason or cash!).

The conversation turns to what tests could be done (apart from phoning the bank) to discover exactly what is and is not held on the card. Each individual throws in different parts of the scene, of their encounters in trying to get cash, statements, balance of accounts, in changing their personal identification number and so on. Slowly there emerges some kind of credible explanation of cash cards, 'rapid cash' tills (where the sum to be withdrawn is entered before the card), why things go wrong, why the card is returned to the customer before the money, why sometimes the balance of account is not available there and then, and so on.

Nor in one sense does it matter that someone, somewhere, knows the answer and could save the trouble of such a debate. We are problem-solving, and in this case we are using a series of group skills — discussing, listening, brainstorming, challenging, co-operating, testing and evaluating each other's ideas, learning from each other and so on. Problems, then, can be conceptual problems, personally constructed, yet group solved. Conceptual problems are very much in the traditions of science: Galileo and Einstein, for example, were much-vaunted exponents of the art of *gedanken* or 'thought experiments' — but more of conceptual problems in other chapters.

THE NATURE OF PROBLEM-SOLVING

Solving problems used to be seen as a particular kind of activity — usually as a major obstacle for pupils, something they found very difficult. For many, solving 'problems' usually meant tackling endless tedious calculations on 'the mole' or the laws of motion. Over time, the problems to be solved have ranged from brain-teasers ('make four squares from these five matchsticks'), IQ-style questions ('what is the next number/letter of the following series . . .'), problems in mathematics (the 'Hanoi Tower' problem), chemistry and physics ('do problems 3 to 13 from Exercise 42 at the back of the book') to larger-scale problems ('design a child's toy that moves around and makes a whirring sound'). More recently there has been an evolution in thinking that has moved the kind of problem away from the closed, single-answer type towards an open-ended, multiple-solution style.

These days, then, the type of problem under consideration has changed and tackling these new problems is becoming acceptable, respectable — even mandatory classroom practice.

In science this move has come about through a combination of several strands: the common commitment to practical activities and 'hands-on' science; a residual influence from 'discovery learning'; and the continuing search for 'relevance' (see the discussion of Stewart, 1987, for example). These come together when youngsters are asked to tackle a practical problem which has no single solution and which can be seen to make use of their scientific understanding in an everyday or industrial/commercial context.

Gagne (1970) suggested that:

> Problem-solving can be viewed as a process by which the learner discovers the combination of previously learned rules that he can apply to achieve a solution for a novel situation . . . but it is also a process that yields new learning.

While I am not an advocate of all Gagne's work, this definition serves to highlight some key points in problem-solving:

- the learner discovers . . .
- previously learned rules . . .
- achieve a solution . . .
- novel situations . . .
- new learning.

That is, the virtues claimed of problem-solving are not only that new knowledge is acquired but that the skills of problem-solving are retained for use in new problems, new situations and new contexts. Skills learned in one context can be carried over and used in a different one. Skills acquired in school are therefore useful for solving more general problems in the outside world — the transfer of learning can be useful. This is the view of Bruner (1961), namely:

> it is only through the exercise of problem solving and the effort of discovery that one learns the working heuristic of discovery, the more one has practice of, the more one is able to generalise what one has learned into a style that serves for any kind of task one may encounter . . .

These are heady claims. At last we may have reached a point where learning in school might actually transfer to everyday life!

PROBLEMS, ALWAYS PROBLEMS . . .

The Standing Conference on Schools Science and Technology (Engineering Council, 1985), for instance, categorizes problems into four basic types: those of a technological nature; ones with a scientific bias; decision-making exercises that include role-play and simulations; and exercises that mainly involve mathematics and language. This is useful, although the distinction between science and technology is not always an easy one to draw.

Here I try to be more specific about the nature of problems and follow Kahney's notion: that a person has a 'problem' when she or he has a goal which cannot be achieved directly (Kahney, 1986). Jackson (1983) summarizes this type of approach as:

$$Problem = Objective + Obstacle$$

It is seldom that there is just one obstacle to solving a problem and the final part of the formula might better read 'obstacles'. Or, if the problem is worked such that one large obstacle is evident, it is always possible to break that up into several smaller parts.

Problems have sometimes been classified as 'open' or 'closed'; 'formal' or 'informal'; or as more or less 'curriculum dedicated' (Munson, 1988). Some have made a distinction between 'free-form' problem-solving and 'goal-orientated' problem-solving. In Chapter 6, I develop this set of distinctions in terms of two contrasting forms of problem-solving, which I have called PS1 and PS2.

Before that, though, it is useful to distinguish between GIVEN problems, where the solver is given both the goal and strategies; GOAL problems, where the solver is given the goal and nothing else—the solvers have to decide and develop their own strategies; and OWN problems, where solvers decide both the goal and the strategies (see, for example, Bentley and Watts, 1989).

In this sense, an arithmetic calculation is very much a problem, but it is specifically a GIVEN problem. The goal is specified and, while all the permissible moves may not be explicit in the problem statement, they are usually clearly defined elsewhere (probably in the preceding pages of the textbook, or in classroom notes).

For GOAL and OWN problems, there are only general principles suggested for problem-solving. Youngsters have to choose the best strategies from a wide range of possibilities to achieve their goal. These general strategies seem to be a combination of 'the design process' and 'the scientific method'. According to Greene (1975), the different levels of problems can be summarized as:

Level 1 — solver already knows solution
Level 2 — solver already knows rules for obtaining solution
Level 3 — solver learns correct solution during the task
Level 4 — solver has to select and evaluate operations for obtaining a solution
Level 5 — solver has to reformulate problem and/or produce some unusual method of solution
Level 6 — solver has to realize that problem exists.

Let's take some examples. This list of twenty questions/problems is one used before (Watts, 1989) but it is useful to indicate a possible range of types. As you browse them, try to categorize the problems, and think about how and why you have allocated them:

1. What are the effects in the immediate environment of acid rain?
2. Use a '555' microchip timer to make a two-tone doorbell, or baby alarm.
3. How can you reduce home heating bills?
4. Make a blind person's or disabled person's gardening tool.
5. How to choose appropriate loudspeakers to match a domestic hi-fi system.
6. Use a computer database to log some data and/or use an interface system to take data readings.
7. Survey the dietary and/or health issues in a local population.
8. Monitor and adjust soil conditions to maximize vegetable growth.
9. Determine fire risks in the home/school environment.
10. Make wine or brew beer from commercially available materials.
11. Create designs through photographic techniques.
12. Survey commercial baby milk.
13. Explore damp control in a house.
14. Investigate a habitat.
15. Measure human amylase activity.
16. Design and construct a light-meter.
17. Examine fading in blue jeans.
18. Explore the effect of people's feet on their environment.
19. Explore the physics of athletes.
20. Investigate the effect on viscosity of stirring a non-drip paint.

Each of the tasks listed here is a problem of one sort of another. However, they are not all the same type of problem. Nor do they include, for instance, the traditional kind of 'problem' from the back of a maths or physics textbook. As noted above, the information necessary to solve this traditional kind of problem is usually provided (the method for solving the problem being somewhere in the text along with one or two 'worked examples') and there is (usually) only one acceptable correct answer. The problems listed above are quite different. Little, if any, relevant information is given, there are only 'best solutions' and few 'right answers', and the methods are not provided. Sometimes there are hints and clues, but no recipes for success. Some of the listed problems can be seen to fall into several different categories: they may be relevant to a traditional science curriculum, be open-ended, yet also be classable as real-life problems.

All the items in the list are problems in the sense that they are tasks which cannot be achieved directly. But they are problems in another sense too. Jackson's formula is 'ends' driven. That is, it seems as if the goal to be reached is, if not the only thing, then certainly the most important part of the activity. While this may be true most of the time, the formula leaves out the 'means' — the methods used to reach the ends. In scientific and technological problem-solving, the means are also important. In life, for instance, it may be possible to 'buy your way' ('cry your way', 'lie your way') out of a problem. While solutions of this nature are interesting from a pragmatic point of view, they are not the kinds of skills-based problem-solving I want to focus on.

OWNING PROBLEMS

Using this terminology, none of the problems in the list are OWN problems — they have all been provided by teachers for pupils. That is not to say that after work has started they do not become 'owned' by the student, simply that they did not start out that way. The most GIVEN of the list is Problem 2. The goal is provided (make a baby alarm, or two-tone door bell) and some of the strategies (use a '555' microchip) are included in the stem of the problem. There are only certain ways in which a '555' microchip can be used and so this prescribes what needs to be done. There is not, however, just one way to do it and so the problem is not entirely fixed. Problem 18 is a good example of a GOAL problem: there are a huge number of ways of sorting through the effect that feet have on the environment.

It is not always possible to get pupils to turn GIVEN problems into OWN problems – they have somehow to reach the point where the problem takes on a particular meaning for them. They have to see it as a problem, which may mean feeling unsettled by it in some way. Solving a problem may include mental, verbal or physical exploration, graphical display or any of a number of responses to the disequilibrium felt.

MORE PROBLEMS

The point of striving for problem ownership in pupils is to enable some of the skills engendered to be transferred into the context of everyday life. In life, for example, a problem might be one of, say, a fifteen-year-old planning a journey. The objective is to travel from central London to visit friends in a small village outside (say) Peterborough. The obstacle is that there may be no single direct way of achieving the objective. The youngster cannot drive him or herself (legally) and so would have to negotiate for a willing (or unwilling) adult to do so. The train service is fast from London to Peterborough, but is relatively expensive and does not service the outlying villages, and so on. The coach service may be slower but cheaper, and may still not cater for small villages. Hitch-hiking is possible but fraught with difficulties. Cycling or walking are possible but barely realistic.

In his book, Kahney (1986) makes a distinction between well-defined problems (ones in which the goal and the possible routes and strategies to a solution are all given at the start) and ill-defined problems (ones in which the goal and the permissible moves have to be supplied by the problem-solver).

Let us consider another list of problems:

1. Make a 'helicopter' from a piece of card 14 cm × 14 cm to spin as far as possible when flicked by a finger from a table top.
2. You are lost in the wilds of a tropical country. You have not drunk anything for three days. All you have around you is some swamp water, some coconut trees and some bamboo trees. You have a sharp knife, some matches and a spare shirt. Find a way of producing pure water from the swamp. You must also find a way of proving it is pure.

3.   Given $f = ma$, where a is $4 \, \text{m s}^{-2}$ and m is $3 \, \text{kg}$, find f.
4.   Why doesn't this typewriter, tape-recorder, etc. work?
5.   What can be done to help infirm or elderly people who find difficulty in pouring boiling water, operating taps, cooker controls, etc?
6.   How can someone be helped to reduce his or her heating bills?
7.   What is pollution? How does it arise? What are the effects of pollution? How is it detected? How is it tackled?
8.   What are the benefits, effects and disadvantages of colour and flavour additives in food?
9.   You are part of a family of five planning to buy a new car. Using technical specifications, draw up the criteria for choice and then choose an appropriate car.
10.   Write a description for a junior-school child about problem-solving.

Compared to arithmetic problems, which are usually well defined, Problem 8 (about additives in food) is ill-defined. Somehow the term 'ill-defined' seems inappropriate, and I return to the distinction already made — it is very much a GOAL problem, where the solver is given the goal and nothing else: the solver has to decide and develop strategies. In this sense, Problem 3 is back to being very much a GIVEN problem. The goal is specified (find f) and, while all the permissible moves are not explicit in the problem statement, they are clearly defined elsewhere. It is not permissible, for example, for the problem-solver to provide the moves and, say, to juxtapose the two figures and write 43 or 34 as a solution.

SKILLS

There are times when it is important to have words tightly defined (in law, for instance) and other times when it is best to leave them loose and vague (in politics?) 'Skill' is a word that has defied comprehensive definition in either way. The easiest thing to say is that 'we know it is hard to define but . . . we know a skill when we see it'. Also, to say that someone has a skill is different from saying that a person is 'skilled' at doing something. The latter has a strong judgemental flavour — to be skilled implies a high level of competence in some activity. These issues are taken up in Chapter 2, where skills are explored more thoroughly. Here, it is worth noting briefly that skills are sometimes referred to in terms such as:

basic skills
higher order skills
core skills
generic skills
life skills

However, people often find it difficult to agree which skills should be called what. For example, basic skills are listed (see Further Education Unit, 1982) as:

language (reading, writing, speaking and listening)
number (calculation, measurement, graphs and tables)
manipulative dexterity and co-ordination
problem-solving
everyday coping
interpersonal relationships
computer literacy
learning

A quick glance shows that these are far from basic skills and contain a myriad more fundamental skills within them (problem-solving, for instance!).

Higher-order skills have been listed as including the ability to:

empathize
motivate self and others
manage groups
manage situations
manage projects/assignments
counsel others

Clearly these are of a different order to those preceding, and the list is potentially endless.

It is not always clear where skills end and processes start. To be able to describe an event accurately is a skill; providing an accurate description is a process. Some (for example, Inner London Education Authority, 1988b) run the two words together and describe things called 'process-skills'. They list:

observing
raising questions
making hypotheses

controlling variables
experimenting
analysing and interpreting communications

On the whole, these are the familiar skills (processes) we know as part of scientific activity.

It is worth trying to identify differences between skills and processes:

- a skill is an individual's contribution to an activity, or towards an objective
- a process is a more general means to an end.

This can raise other sorts of difficulties and these are discussed in Chapter 2. It is worth noting that the purpose of problem-solving in schools can be two-fold: it is sometimes to apply the skills youngsters have developed, and it is sometimes aimed at developing the skill itself.

TRANSFER

The process of transfer is discussed more fully in Chapter 4. Here it deserves just a brief mention. I have already singled out Problem 3 in the list above for comment. It is worth some further discussion because it is a very common type of problem in schools. The approved strategy for teaching and learning this kind of problem-solving is quite straightforward: the textbook usually contains sections where principles are defined, discussed and elaborated with a few 'worked examples'. There then follows a section of similar practice problems for the student to do. As Kahney (1986) suggests, this approach is based on the notion that students can learn to extract general principles from problem-solving experiences, which they can apply to solve other similar problems: it is the 'drill and practice' routine. This is a time-honoured teaching method and we know that in some circumstances it works. Doing example after example, all of which vary in only a small degree (by changing, say, the numbers), can lead to new instances of the problem being solved quickly and easily. Is that not how we learn to add and subtract, 'do' fractions, or even learn to drive a car? As a problem arises in road traffic we surely do not need to revisit all the skills we have—we want to be able to use them quickly, efficiently and automatically. And that comes about through practice in lots of similar circumstances.

This raises a multitude of questions, though, such as:

- are there underlying-principle skills involved in problems that can be extracted (by the teacher or the student) so that solutions can be transferred to other problems?
- are these skills/processes the same for *all* problems or are there different types of problem and, therefore, ways of finding solutions?
- can these principles be taught and, if so, how?
- does that teaching (in this case) lie within science education or is it a cross-curricular issue?

WHY PROBLEM-SOLVE?

I have been hinting at a series of answers to this question. For example:

- problem-solving enables youngsters to take ownership of a task
- it encourages decision-making and many social skills
- it is a form of both active learning and discovery learning
- it is a vehicle for teaching many scientific skills, and for reaching the content aspects of science
- it allows cross-curricular activity
- it provides relevance and real-life contexts
- problem-solving and creative thinking are among the highest and most complex forms of human activity
- it enhances communication.

However, the central message of the book is the first: the pivotal virtue of problem-solving is as a means of transferring some of the responsibility and ownership for learning to the learner. It is about the pupils making decisions — within limits. As Rob Johnsey (1986) says:

> If the problems we set require the children to make choices, then we can be assured that they are thinking for themselves. Making decisions about a solution of a problem is a creative activity and often the end product will be an expression of the child's personality. Furthermore, if the solution works or is at least partially effective, the child will gain in confidence to tackle further problems. We must therefore use our skills as teachers to set problems that stretch the imagination of the child but at the same time lie within his or her sphere of ability.

The main point of adopting the approach in schools is that the emphasis is on the learner using a planned approach (the learner's or someone else's) to tackle a problem. It becomes the learner's responsibility to delineate the problem, decide on what an appropriate solution might be, derive and test possible solutions, and choose the point at which the problem appears solved. The problem might be one that is presented to the solver, or one generated by his or her own thinking, actions or lifestyle. If youngsters are not engaged in setting the goal and working out the routes and strategies for themselves, they may not see the goal as worth achieving. Then the problem disappears; it becomes an irrelevance.

The adoption of problem-solving activities in school science courses is happening quite slowly. Early work in schools (for example, by Mathews *et al.*, 1981) was a useful attempt to simulate and explore the roles of scientists 'doing' science. It is increasingly seen as a valuable way of providing more open learning situations where youngsters are less constrained by didactic teaching methods (Bentley and Watts, 1989).

Managing problem-solving in the classroom raises further questions:

- do you set the same problem for a whole class group so that different pupils generate different solutions?
- do you set one large problem for all and ask different groups to tackle different aspects so that you build up a composite picture at the end?
- do you set different problems for different groups, or even a different problem for each individual, and allow them to work separately?
- before beginning problem-solving, do you first deliberately teach all the facts, concepts and skills so that the pupils will have all the relevant information at their fingertips?
- or do you use the motivating power of problem-solving as a means of allowing the pupils to decide and satisfy their own knowledge needs?

PROBLEM-SOLVING AND THE NATIONAL CURRICULUM

It was noted earlier that, in science, the term 'problem-solving' has moved from meaning the solution of mathematical calculations, or logical puzzles, to being a byword for activity-based learning. There are good reasons to suppose that this notion of 'problem-solving' will survive the next few years:

- it is firmly embedded in the rhetoric, if not the practice, of science and technological education. This appears, for example, in text books, curriculum documents and examination board rubric.
- it tops the list in the 'pedagogic shift' towards participative group work, away from didactic methods. It did so, for example, in 'Science Education 5–16' (Department of Education and Science, 1985), which probably presages much of what has been said in the National Curriculum.

The Further Education Unit (1986) sees problem-solving as a major way of integrating science and technology, as do Black and Harrison (1985). The Engineering Council (1985) recommends problem-solving for primary-school science while, probably more important, it features in the coursework assessment for most GCSE boards.

On this evidence, problem-solving has had a relatively good press compared with other types of teaching and learning approach. With the introduction of the National Curriculum, problem-solving has almost become 'institutionalized' into parts of the curriculum. While this institutionalizing could have been extended further, the political will to do so was missing. However, the state of the curriculum art is as follows. Many (most?) of the Attainment Targets and Programmes of Study outlined in the Science National Curriculum are prefaced by the words 'investigate' and 'explore'. The discussions that precede these statements are based on a very strong child-centred, constructivist (Watts and Pope, 1989) model which sees the pupil undertaking much of the discovery and practical work involved — it is the pupil who, on the whole, is expected to investigate and explore, not the teacher.

When choosing which learning experiences to devise for classes, teachers are exhorted (National Curriculum Council, 1989a) to satisfy such criteria as:

> Will the experience give opportunity to apply scientific ideas and skills to real life problems, including those which require a technological solution?

Another answer, then, to the question 'why do problem-solving?' might be 'because it is part of the National Curriculum'. A key requirement of the National Curriculum is that pupils should be encouraged to develop their investigative skills and their understanding of science through systematic experimentation and investigations which (by age 13) are to be:

> set within the everyday experience of pupils and in wider contexts, and which require the deployment of previously encountered concepts and their investigative skills to solve practical problems;

and, by age 16, are to be:

> set in the everyday experience of pupils and in novel contexts, involving increasingly abstract concepts and the application of knowledge, understanding and skills, where pupils need to make decisions about the degree of precision and safe working required.

The guidelines to the National Curriculum (National Curriculum Council, 1989) go on to require:

- pupils to plan and carry through investigations in which they may have to vary more than one key variable and where the variable to be measured can be treated continuously
- pupils to make strategic decisions about the number, range and accuracy of measurements, and select and use appropriate apparatus and instruments,

and that science work should:

- promote invention and creativity.

In the main, Attainment Target 1 is the main reference point for problem-solving activity. For example, at level 6 youngsters are required to:

> contribute to the analysis and investigation of a collaborative exercise in which outcomes are derived from the results of a number of different lines of inquiry, possibly including experimentation, survey and use of secondary sources, in the context of which each pupil should:
>
> - use experience and knowledge to make predictions in new contexts
> - identify and manipulate two discrete independent variables and control other variables
> - prepare a detailed written plan, where the key variables are named and details of the experimental procedure are given
> - record data in tables and translate it into appropriate graphical forms
> - produce reports which include a critical evaluation of certain features of the experiment, such as reliability, validity of measurements and experimental design.

The emphasis on investigation and exploration in the National Curriculum is very positive. When this is coupled to the requirements that youngsters operate in groups, adopting a number of roles within such groups, that they should plan, carry out and report on such investigations, then we are almost there. Many such investigations could be at the level of GOAL and GIVEN problems and could resemble some of the problems in the lists presented above. The will to move to OWN problems is a natural, but difficult, step from there.

INCORPORATING PROBLEM-SOLVING INTO THE CURRICULUM

Let us consider how problem-solving is and might be in the curriculum by considering two dimensions. The first of these represents the extent of problem-solving in the curriculum. At one extreme, the whole school curriculum could be based on problem-solving; at the other extreme just some (a few) lessons would involve problem-solving, where the problems are geared just to the subject area concerned. 'Curriculum-dedicated' problems is a term devised by Munson (1988).

The two extremes of this dimension are not so far-fetched. The left-hand 'pole' of the dimension (see Figure 1.1) suggests that schooling could all be built around a problem-solving approach: hints of this occur, for instance, in Black and Harrison (1985) and the National Curriculum Technology Working Party report (National Curriculum Council, 1989b). The other pole is much more rooted in practice and identifies the way teachers generate problems that are clearly drawn from the issues within the curriculum being attended to at any particular moment.

Figure 1.1 Dimension one: the extent of problem-solving in the curriculum.

Figure 1.2   Dimension two: the diversity of problem-solving applications.

The second dimension represents the diversity of problem-solving applications. At one extreme is the idea that problem-solving concerns a wide variety of problems; at the other is the feeling that problems are solely technological 'make and do' ones (see Figure 1.2). Some people do populate the extremes and so the ideas are worth charting.

Back to the first dimension; it is, presumably, possible to devise a succession of problems which will occupy youngsters profitably throughout their time in school, and 'deliver' all the knowledge, understanding, skills and processes they will need in their school lives. Probably no school anywhere operates like this, but there are some (certainly in Japan) that have gone some way towards it. It represents, perhaps, the 'problem-solver's dream school'. The other end of the dimension is much more common – schools and curricula where there is little (or no) problem-solving taking place (and then only in a few restricted circumstances: the 'problem-solver's nightmare').

The second dimension simply represents a separation between people who see that there is a huge range of possible problems to be solved – problems come in all shapes and sizes. Such people differ from those who see problems only within design and technology (or any other single subject matter) – and there are many who do see only problems in their own field! Presumably most people can site themselves somewhere on both dimensions and take a non-extreme view; but that, too, has implications! A mid-point position would say that it is possible to undertake a substantial part of the whole school curriculum through problem-solving, using a fairly wide range of problem types in a variety of subject areas. That is a long way from how schools currently deliver their curriculum. To try to achieve this might be a short-term aim for some, but it would be a (very) long-term goal for many. Perhaps there is a ladder of short- and long-term aims.

Putting the dimensions at right-angles gives a two-by-two matrix (Figure 1.3). The first quadrant represents what is probably the most usual state of affairs, where problem-solving is restricted to a few kinds of problem in specialized subject areas. This is often the case in secondary schools in science, CDT (craft, design and technology) or home economics, where the subject areas do not always know

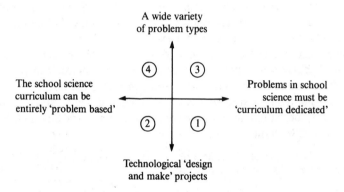

Figure 1.3 Two-dimensional matrix representing both the extent and the diversity of problem-solving applications.

what each other is doing. Quadrants two and three are mid ways out of this — where problems are spread across the curriculum and/or problem types are seen to be wide and varied. Quadrant four is idealistic, but represents a goal to work for. Presumably, if what is wanted is young people who are free-standing, self-directive, confident and purposeful finders-of-solutions to a range of problems, then this is where we should be heading.

PROBLEM-SOLVING AND THE SCIENCE CURRICULUM

A range of curriculum materials currently on the market is beginning to introduce problem-solving into lessons. Science Horizons (Hudson *et al.*, 1987), for example, is a primary science course which introduces a number of problem-solving situations; Peacock (1986) sets out deliberately to do so, and Fisher's useful book (Fisher, 1987) is directed specifically at primary work. There is some material directed at lower secondary school science, for example, in Science in Process (Inner London Education Authority, 1988a) and Warwick Process Science (Screen, 1986), and in the SATIS material. Some has been developed at local level and can be accessed through the Secondary Science Curriculum Review (Secondary Science Curriculum Review, 1987a, 1987b) or Heaney and Watts (1988).

At GCSE there have been a number of moves to incorporate problem-solving into coursework and practical assessments. Here, problem-solving is seen as the most advanced set of skills to be attained, the 'culmination of the course' as Sparkes and Soper (1988) say of GCSE biology:

> All other aims and assessment objectives can only be leading to this ultimate of the scientific process.

The teaching of problem-solving is raised in other chapters.

SCIENCE AND TECHNOLOGY

One possible reading of the National Curriculum documents and discussions is that, soon, 'all teachers must become teachers of technology'. At a time of rapid change in schools a clear lead is required in order to establish curriculum coherence in science and technology. Such an initiative might be based on the notion of 'extended problem-solving' and has been argued and urged by Black and Harrison (1985), for example.

In school technology, the emphasis is often upon hardware, not software, solutions. Science is often the reverse – the emphasis is on paper solutions, not actual artefacts. To link the two approaches, there is a need for course-based material that promotes curriculum coherence through 'design-and-make' activities, extended project work, conceptual and physical modelling, and 'real-world' problems – extended problem-solving. Throughout, there needs to be a strong emphasis on both scientific and technological skills, processes and problem-solving approaches.

The differences between science and technology are slight and may sometimes be a difference of emphasis rather than substance. Of school science and technology Johnsey (1986) says:

> One [set of processes] is that of the pure scientist in which a question is posed and answered by experiment. The other is the process of design technology involving the solution to a problem by the design and construction of a device.

The two processes are shown as Figures 1.4 and 1.5.

Liaison between technology and science (and other subject areas) in schools ranges from 'cross-border' co-operation through an uneasy détente to, in some cases, outright hostility. This is a point raised in Chapter 5. However, as Rowlands (1987) says:

> A comparison of the aims of science and CDT courses will readily reveal a number of areas of overlap, especially in the teaching of technology. There are clear statements in the GCSE National Criteria for physics, biology, science and chemistry that technology and socio-economic applications of the subject should be allocated 15% of the available marks. In addition, the physics criteria allow for the possibility of up to 20% of the total marks coming from project work which could well involve technological activity, which will form an integral part of all GCSE CDT courses. Material which can be used in science to give pupils experience of 'technological activity' may serve the same purpose in the CDT area of the curriculum.

Nor is CDT the only area where technology — and problem-solving — takes place. For example, some work has been done to develop problem-solving in health education, home economics, history, English, IT and other subject areas.

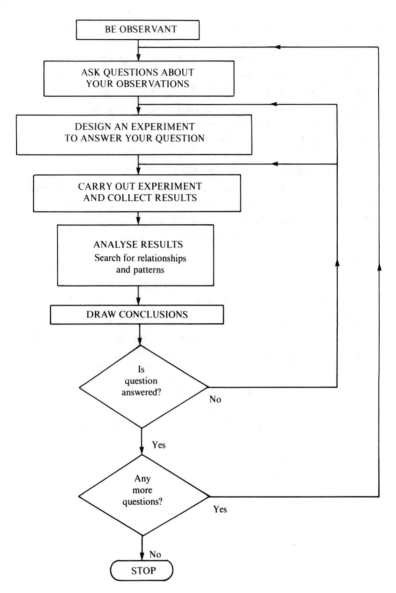

Figure 1.4   The science process. Source: Johnsey (1986)

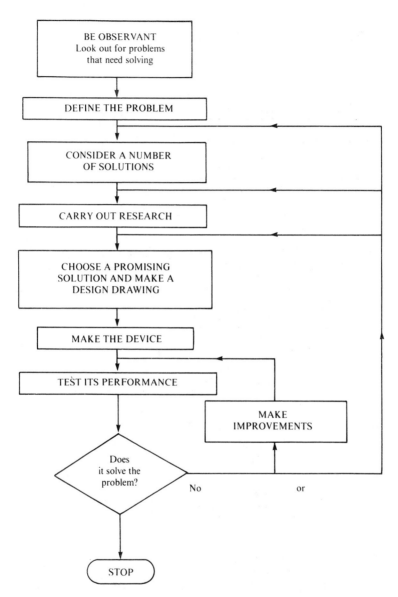

Figure 1.5 The problem-solving process. Source: Johnsey (1986).

Chapter 2

Skills, Processes and Methods of Problem-Solving

This chapter looks at models for the problem-solving approach, including issues of experiential learning. It considers how one might detail the skills and processes implicit in a problem-solving approach, and how these can be managed.

INTRODUCTION

Chapter 1 presented a brief look at such terms as 'problem', 'skill' and 'ownership'. This chapter has two main points. First it considers the 'problem-solving approach' and what that means in practice. Saying *the* problem solving approach implies that there is only one, or only one important approach. This is both right and wrong — there is one method which is described repeatedly, but this is not the only (or necessarily the most workable) method. Second, the focus in the chapter is on skills and processes in problem-solving generally and how these relate to problem-solving in the classroom.

METHODS OF SOLVING PROBLEMS

There is a primary issue at stake here. We need to distinguish between general approaches to solving problems (and how we introduce pupils and students to these) and the particular individual methods that people use to solve specific problems (and how we can counsel problem-solvers as they do that). First, there has been much written about 'the problem-solving approach', which is, in essence, an ideal way of working. This is the approach most often held up as the model for the way that pupils *should* work then solving problems. However, second, there is also a lot of research about how people actually *do* solve problems. On the whole, they do so by a variety of different ways, seldom by the classic prescribed method. The task in the classroom is to reconcile the two: to offer a general structure for how youngsters might tackle problems, while also helping them to sort through the tasks inherent within a particular problem to be solved.

It is worth taking the popularly prescribed method apart if only to see how it can be improved and implemented in the classroom.

THE 'POPULAR' PROBLEM-SOLVING APPROACH

The first thing to note is that 'methods' and 'processes' are linked roughly as follows:

$$\text{method} = \text{sum of processes}$$
$$\text{process} = \text{sum of skills}$$

Processes are usually represented as a cycle, or loop, which goes through the following general processes:

hypothesizing
experimenting
designing
evaluating
recording
interpreting
communicating

Williams and Jinks (1985), for instance, talk, in terms of primary classrooms, of the 'design line' (see Figure 2.1). The 'design line' helps, they say, by separating the journey into a number of stages. On the diagram, (1) is where the process starts. This is often referred to as a 'need'. Stage (2) is the generation of a large number of ideas — as divergent and creative as possible. Stage (3) is the research stage, gathering information and details on the problem so as to make a selection of the ideas for a solution. Stage (4) is the choice of a preferred idea, which is constructed (5) and tested (6). The solution is then evaluated (7) and is modified or accepted as seen fit.

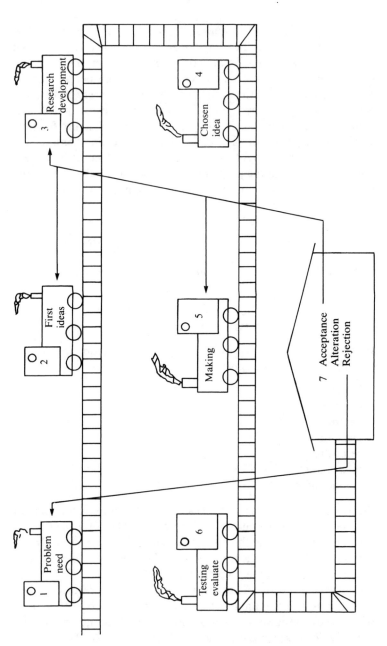

Figure 2.1   The 'design line'. Source: Williams and Jinks (1985).

At secondary level, the Assessment of Performance Unit (1984) list several similar stages:

Ia Generation of the problem and a genuine perception of its meaning.

Ib Reformulation into a form open to investigation.

II Detailed planning of the experimental work.

III Carrying out the experiment.

IV Recording the results in an appropriate form.

V Interpreting the results and drawing conclusions.

VI Evaluation.

The stages are not always linear, but can loop back at different points, as shown in their diagram (Figure 2.2). Similar looped systems are used in CDT, for example, Page *et al.* (1982), and in psychology. For instance, Lovejoy (1988) recommends the ZAP technique for psychology students:

1. Headline: students state problem.
2. Analysis: they make notes about the problem, ask questions about it, clarify the problem for themselves.
3. Springboard: a brainstorming session for ideas on how to tackle it, possible routes and solutions, the constraints that are evident.
4. Selection: begin to sort ideas one at a time, choosing a few of the most plausible.
5. Paraphrase: re-sort the problems so that all involved can agree a procedure and the tasks to be done.
6. Check responses: monitor actions as they begin to take shape; perhaps go back to the drawing board at this stage.
7. Evaluate solutions: qualify success.

As suggested earlier, these kinds of processes, stages or loops are an idealized format and few problem-solvers would say they followed it exactly, although in retrospect they might be able to identify the main stages in their activities. One trouble with trying to set out processes like this is that they give the appearance of being real and fixed. It is undoubtedly possible to watch and talk to many problem-solvers both as they solve problems and when finished, and to categorize their actions in this way. However, people are seldom (if ever) as regular and clear as this — there is no mention here of intuition, hunches, a flash of inspiration, doggedness, perseverance,

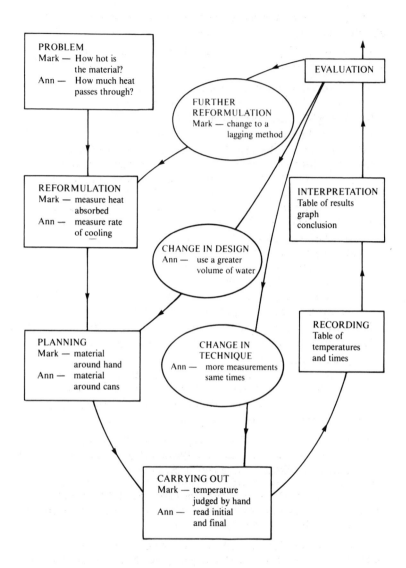

Figure 2.2 'Pupils' problem-solving activities, exemplified in 'Survival'.
Source: Assessment of Performance Unit (1984).

necessity, frustration, elegance, simplicity, extravagance and so on — all of which contribute in some measure to what is going on. Before a more detailed look at creativity and invention, let us take a more expansive view of some of the processes in the cycles above.

Formulating the problem: 'needs analysis'

Where do problems come from? At one level, problems are all around us all of the time and come from personal preferences, values and ambitions. Fisher (1987), for instance, encourages youngsters to ask the questions:

Why do you think that . . .?
What do you notice when . . .?
What do you mean by . . .?
Is there another way?
What would happen if?
Can you show me how?
Will it always work?
What might explain it?
Which explanation is best?
How can you test it?

From these sorts of question problems surely arise. Carl Sagan says in the preface of Stephen Hawking's *A Brief History of Time* (Hawking, 1988):

Except for children (who don't know enough not to ask the important questions) few of us spend much time wondering why nature is the way it is. . . . There are even children, and I have met some of them, who want to know what a black hole looks like; what is the smallest piece of matter; why we remember the past and not the future; how it is, if there was chaos early, that there is apparently order today; and why there IS a universe.

At a second level, problems arise from very specific issues: how to move a tree torn down by high winds; how to take an aerial photograph of the school; how to pipe crude oil at low temperatures; how to maximize the growth of vegetables in given conditions; and so on. A favourite problem arose from a thirteen-year-old who wanted to know if the gerbils in the cage at the back of the classroom behaved in the same way when no one was there as they did when a class of thirty was there (and many more around the building). The problem centred on what might be taken as indicators of 'behaviour' or 'activity', and how these could be monitored when no one was there – over a weekend, for example. This same problem has been used with groups of teachers and has provoked both fierce debate and ingenious solutions.

One possible strategy to raise problems is to ask a group to think of individuals less fortunate than themselves. In what way do their fortunes differ? Are there small ways in which their plights can be alleviated? Do some of their problems have a technological solution? What might these be? For example, a whole year group in a school was given the opportunity of extended problem-solving work around the theme of 'how to improve the life of an eighty-six-year-old woman'.

There is always a need for classroom teachers to build a bank of problems, preferably ones raised by youngsters in the course of lessons. However, there are now readily available banks of questions and some sources appear at the end of the book as Appendix 2. The idea of the 'problem bank' is discussed again later.

Reformulation

Problem-solvers can either define their own problem and set out OWN sub-goals for themselves, or they can be presented with a GIVEN or GOAL task. Either way, having established a problem area, this now needs to be refined. For instance:

- there needs to be a clear definition of the problem – or attention must be fixed on a particular goal;
- this needs to be reformulated into a manageable form, or into an empirical form. This is sometimes referred to as coming to terms with the 'problem space'.

This is sometimes done in a group by 'talking through the problem': deciding on the nature of the task, the general limitations, the constraints, the various facets or sub-goals it might contain, similar problems that have been solved before and so on. Individuals – fixing a car, for example – are often to be seen simply fiddling with leads, connections, prodding, poking, knocking, etc., before they actually set about tackling the problem. There may be no real point to the fiddling, beyond speculative trial-and-error. However, such activity is often deeper than that and constitutes an important part of problem-solving: it can often be a private, tacit way of sorting out the size of the problem and the scope for solving it – of exploring what might be called 'the problem space'. The fiddling can also be a way of obtaining information about the problem, receiving feedback, sensing what size of adjustments can be made, developing a 'feel' for what can be done.

It is important for this stage to be encouraged. For instance, youngsters can sometimes jump into a problem task with tremendous enthusiasm but without much forethought of what is manageable. They can then become locked into an over-ambitious project or trapped in a blind alley, with disheartening results.

The 'problem space' is important because is is a notion of the scale of the problem, of the size of the tasks involved. It is not unusual for people to say 'I had no idea of what I was getting into'; 'I was only barely able to scratch the surface'; 'It was only when I thought I had finished that I realized what I should have been doing all along'.

Generating ideas

The personal 'fiddling' is often the time needed to think up and reject (or accept) a range of solutions. In a group this is easier because there are so many more brains to storm, and one idea can beget another. As a technique, brainstorming can be taught. This is dis-cussed, for instance, in Ellington (1987) and in Bentley and Watts (1989), along with the teaching of other skills. There are different forms of brainstorming and some are suitable for:

- individuals or groups
- at the start
- while the work is in progress.

Ideas should include both sensible and silly ones. Crazy ideas should be encouraged – they can often pave the way for the more sensible ones, or produce unorthodox solutions (when someone asks 'well, why *not* do it that way?). The humorous solution and the 'anything goes' mood can produce quirky ways of tackling the problem. Ideas can tumble out by 'slippage' or malapropism (see a longer discussion in Chapter 4). Even if not providing the final solution, this might set up some connections for others who see a different way of approaching the problem. In this sense, ideas can be produced which are variations on a theme.

A real example might help. The problem set for some sixth-form scientists was that of taking an aerial photograph of the school. The main piece of apparatus was a very cheap, lightweight and disposable camera from a well-known high-street retailer. It is fairly robust, has twelve exposures, and the camera is broken up to remove the film when used. The brainstorming sessions could have lasted too long, in an otherwise constrained time slot in the day, and so this had to be sharply focused and then the ideas sifted quickly.

The groups sorted swiftly into 'helium balloonists', 'kite flyers' and 'other', and they each set about sorting out tasks so that the camera could be raised off the ground and then triggered at the appropriate position. The brainstorming had generated a vast number of ideas and two students (who were the 'other' group) decided to carry on thinking, despite being urged otherwise, before jumping into the task. As it happened, and by what must have been pure coincidence, their pictures were the successful ones. They rejected the sophistication of balloons and kites, and opted for the simplicity of heartily throwing the camera very high into the air and allowing it to parachute down. The shutter was released by a simple timing device, which they set according to what they thought would be the travel time upwards. In practice, the parachute was not always successful in providing a soft landing and one of the two had to be stationed to catch it.

Their extra thinking time allowed them to try a variation of the themes of the other groups. They had overheard one comment about trying to 'shoot' the camera upwards, translated this as 'chute' the camera, and their idea was born. Note, this was not cheating but good lateral thinking.

One of the most difficult tasks, it seems, is to teach someone how to be innovative or creative. There is a view that one either has or does not have creativity — it cannot be taught. I do not subscribe to this view, and discussions of teaching innovative thinking and creative ways of working are tackled later.

Graphicacy time

Some people can generate ideas better by playing (mentally, or on paper) with variable conditions — varying one condition at a time, and then several together. This is time for 'idea drawing', 'doodles', 'saying what you mean on paper' or making rough sketches; it helps to sharpen ideas, enhance communication, provide some scale and reduce the number of possible solutions, as well as to flesh out the 'problem space'. These kinds of process can give the less imaginative in the group time to gather their thoughts.

Again, this is a stage to be encouraged. Rough sketches can give rise to other ideas, clarification and indicate solutions. All told, though, the 'ideas stage' should have a finite end — possibly with the promise of more 'think time' later.

Research stage

This is another stage to be encouraged: reading reference books to see how the problem has been tackled before. The information need not be in books, of course, but on video tapes, interactive video discs, films, cassettes and so on — or be housed in the expertise of other people. Research, though, also means doing some preliminary testing. So, if the problem is about thermal insulation, or bridge building in the classroom, it will be important to pre-test some properties of materials to see if they will do the job.

Rowlands (1987) says, quite rightly, that:

> Research skills are an important facet of problem solving activities. It is not intended that pupils, in isolation and unaided, should produce solutions to the problems. The development of a set of resource materials linked to each topic or sub-topic will go a long way to ensure the successful use of problem solving material.

As any librarian will note, literature research skills are developed over time and need practice. Youngsters do not automatically know how to access relevant data from text and need to be taught how to best achieve that. Important, too, is that teachers take time both to teach research skills and to ensure that the relevant literature is accessible. In particular, they need to:

- check that the materials available are adequate for what is wanted;
- check the content of the resources;
- collect a variety of resources;
- encourage the students to explore the topic fully;

- discourage them from copying directly from the material, but encourage them in adapting it in some way;
- encourage variety in presentation; foster self-evaluation as regards the students' work.

Experimenting, the design stage, solving the problem

This is the 'doing' stage. All the ideas, hints, research and reformulation must lead to one or a few testable options, which become the kernel of the planned solution. In school technology it is called the 'planning and making', or the realization stage. Again, this is often seen to be one stage, but more probably encompasses a range of moves as some solution is brought into focus.

The 'popular' problem-solving method is an ideal form, but there are limits to its usefulness. First, although people who solve problems can recognize some of the stages as they proceed with their task, they do not necessarily pass through all of them, nor do they necessarily pass through them only once. Second, some people solve problems by other methods—for instance, by trial and error, sharp lateral thinking and so on. This is much more difficult to teach, and so the 'popular' method helps to structure our approach in the classroom—but be aware that some youngsters will take short cuts and long cuts. And this is to be encouraged.

The major difficulty with the idea of a chain or cycle of problem-solving processes is that in practice it can never be so linear. For example, some texts in technology begin with 'the problem' and then go through a sequence of 'formulation', 'ideas', 'developing the ideas', 'construction', 'refinement' and 'evaluation'. It is hard to understand how the problem can be formulated before any idea of whether or how it might be tackled. Instead it is often the ideas that generate the problem in the first place.

THE STRUCTURED SERENDIPITY METHOD OF PROBLEM-SOLVING

The term 'Structured Serendipity' is simply a fancy title I have given to the process of trying to maximize carry-over from known situations to unknown problems. It is less of a problem-solving method itself than an acceptance that such models cannot be rigorous. It is, therefore, an attempt to make 'methods' more free and inventive, and relies on four major points:

1. There is seldom enough time – or resources – to be able to give full reign to the 'popular' problem-solving method.
2. Teach for problem-solving early and regularly – it needs specific skills and approaches.
3. Problems are better solved if they are generated by the solver, i.e. if they are OWN problems.
4. Problems are more easily solved if they seem similar to ones that have been successfully solved before.

Much of this is raised in future chapters but a brief outline is in order here. The first point concerns the time necessary for all the stages in the 'popular' method described so far. Most school sessions take place in slot lasting an hour or so, a morning if lucky, a whole day if very fortunate. To tackle all the stages fully requires a long time – most groups when actually solving a problem short-circuit many of the stages. For instance, they do not do the research, or, more likely, they rely on their own knowledge as it is at the time. Once started on a solution, they seldom make and test several prototypes (if any) – they go all out for the full-blown resolution in one go. Moreover, their evaluation is seldom serious, let alone returning through the loop to repeat the process in order to modify or refine the solution. As Gilbert (1987) says of her class:

> The children apparently had no concept of the scientific cycle of experimentation and improvement, they were totally geared to things working first time.

The main reason always given by adults is lack of resources, usually time. This raises an important point: each problem has an in-built cost–benefit factor. No matter how intriguing (unless it is the kind of compulsive problem like that presented by a Rubik cube) the problem-solver will weigh up the time commitment and decide quite quickly how much effort to devote to the task. After that, whatever solution has emerged will have to do.

The second point seems self-evident. Building up a reservoir of problem-solving skills needs time and practice; the sooner started the better. Parts of the problem-solving process must therefore be taught at an early stage.

The third point is about the ownership of the problems. The tasks do not have to be provided by the teacher. Hadfield (1987), for instance, notes that in problem-orientated structured teaching, it is the task of the teacher to structure the material in such a way that problem-solving situations arise in the course of lessons. So, although the context is that which is provided by the teacher, the problems themselves are generated by the class.

The final point is that problems do not always have to be tackled from first principles each time. Problem-solving in one context must be seen as appropriate for use in another context. As Gilbert (1987) says of her own informal study of problem-solving with young children:

> problem solving exercises must be directly and obviously applicable to any previous discoveries, or the children may be confused by the change of direction, discard the previous information as useless and give up any attempt to reason for themselves.

So, what has been learned in one session must be seen to be applicable in another so that the carry-over is maximized.

The Structured Serendipity approach to problem-solving, then, is an attempt to encourage problem-solvers to maximize their transfer from one context to the next. In essence its general strategies might be (in no particular order):

- To look for analogous problems — what is the current problem like? What does it remind me of? Have I read/heard/seen anything like it at all before? How was that problem solved? What similarities are there with what has gone before.
- Once an analogous problem has been recognized the solution must be translated into a solution for the target problem. How can it be applied to the next problem? Is there any carry-over at all?
- Look to see how other people have solved (or are solving) the same (or similar) problems. Best of all, find and mimic an expert as he or she solves a similar problem.
- Solvers might develop a series of partial solutions to the target problem. Successive partial solutions can serve as a framework for modifying the most recent partial solution to produce a new one. That is, to break the problem down into sub-goals and be flexible about how you move from one sub-solution to the next without losing sight of the overall goal.
- Hints are readily available in real-world problems. Problem-

solvers in this method must draw on vicariously acquired knowledge as hard as they can. As Rowlands (1987) says of classroom problem-solving:

> Even with carefully selected material, it would be unrealistic to expect the majority of pupils to solve a problem without appropriate help from the teacher. There are pupils who, when given a difficult problem, are able to solve it methodically with no assistance from the teacher. However, most groups will need guidance and it is the gauging of when and where to give the advice, clue or hint which is so crucial. To give too little help could leave the group struggling and disheartened and remove any confidence the pupils might have in solving future problems. To give too much help could take away the satisfaction pupils might feel upon successfully solving a problem.

Rowlands continues by suggesting that the best type of clue is where pupils use readily available resources to research possible solutions. The resources could include:

library books
magazines
video programmes
photographs/slide sets
posters
diagrams
models

- Work backwards/work forwards, moving between the start position and the goal, sometimes working back from the goal, sometimes working from the start forward. This leads to a kind of means/ends analysis. That is, determining the 'differences' between a current state of a problem and a goal state — differences between what you have now and what you want to end up with. The moves then are aimed at finding operators to reduce the difference. This operates principally by analysing goals into subgoals and working out which moves will get closer to the target. It is a very useful strategy in real-life circumstances.
- What Kahney (1986) calls a Heuristic Search. Heuristics are 'rules of thumb' methods which often succeed but which do not guarantee a solution to a problem. A mundane heuristic might be 'ask for directions when lost in an unfamiliar place'.

The awkward truth here is that solving problems this way relies heavily on what is already known and not on fresh knowledge. That makes the structured Serendipity method an alternative approach;

not one to be used instead of the 'popular' method but as well as it. Then it allows old skills/new skills, old knowledge/new knowledge to be deployed. Gagne (1970), for instance, says:

> The results of using rules in problem solving are not confined to achieving a goal, satisfying as that may be for the thinker. When problem solution is achieved, something is also learned, in the sense that the individual's capability is more or less permanently changed. What emerges from problem solving is a higher order rule, which becomes part of the individual's repertory. The class of situation, when encountered again may be responded to with greater facility by means of recall and is no longer looked on as a problem. Problem solving, then, must definitely be considered a form of learning.

SKILLS

Chapter 1 contained a brief look at skills and what they might be. There seems to be a wide diversity of opinion as to what exactly constitutes a skill and, more importantly, whether or not there is a hierarchy of skills, from the simple to the complex. Here, I want to deal with the skills and processes involved in problem-solving and how (if at all) we can use problem-solving to maximize skill training.

In Chapter 1 the distinction between a skill and a process was introduced: a skill is an individual's contribution to an activity, or towards an objective; a process is a general means to an end. The problem, of course, is that it is not always so easy to separate the two in practice. The Further Education Unit (1982) suggests that skills require perception, decision-making, knowledge, judgements and understanding; at the same time all skills involve some kind of co-ordinated, overt activity by hands, of speech, etc. It rejects, for instance, the notion that skills are simply the ability to perform some manipulative occupational task.

Certainly, a skill is a capacity or a competence, the ability to successfully perform a task of some kind, whether intellectual or manual. Rather than try to determine a hierarchy of 'low order' or 'high order' skills, I prefer to focus on specific and general skills. Some skills may be restricted in their use to a small number of instances, others may be applicable in a variety of contexts. Often skills can be identified in clusters (for instance, social skills). There are clearly degrees of skilfulness, and the assessment of people's skills needs to be considered at the level appropriate to the skill in question.

Consequently, the skills involved in problem-solving will depend on the problem, the context in which it is set and the possible routes to a solution. Trying to assess whether or not skills have been deployed successfully will depend on their role in solving the problem. Initially, it is possible to identify some broad groups of skills, for example:

- *Problem-solving and creative skills*:
  The ability to diagnose the features of a problem, to frame hypotheses, design experiments to test them and evaluate the results; the ability to draw on relevant ideas and use materials inventively.
- *Observation and visual skills*:
  The ability to observe accurately; the ability to record distributions, patterns and relationships, using scale, perspective, shape and colour; and the ability to interpret observations.
- *Numerical skills*:
  The ability to estimate and measure, and to understand the use of numerical relationships, shape and patterns.
- *Imaginative skills*:
  The ability to put oneself into other situations, whether of time, place or person, to visualize other experiences; the ability to discipline the imagination by evidence and experience, to reorder and reshape experiences and images.
- *Organizational and study skills*:
  The ability to extract information, to arrange in sequence, to classify, to weigh and interpret evidence and to draw conclusions, to see relationships; the ability to make the best use of time.
- *Physical and practical skills*:
  The ability to develop manual dexterity and a variety of co-ordinated body movements, to select appropriate tools and items of equipment and to use them effectively.
- *Social skills*:
  The ability to co-operate, to negotiate, to express ideas in a variety of contexts, to consider other points of view, to recognize non-verbal communications.
- *Communication skills*:
  The ability to use reading and writing, oral, aural, non-verbal and graphical skills to receive and convey communications without the risk of misunderstanding.

Beyond this, it is possible to isolate more particular skills. For instance, in Watts and Michell (1987) we included for science in schools:

Processes like:
- communicating and discussing, which includes questioning, thinking, seeking help, negotiating, listening;
- processes of information, which include selecting, using relationships, designing, drawing conclusions, controlling interacting variables;
- problem-solving, experimentation and decision-making, which include predicting, inferring, interpreting, formulating hypotheses, modelling, evaluating, assessing, classifying, managing time, costing.

Skills like:
listening, talking, reading, drawing, numeracy, small group skills, observing, non-verbal communication, searching, measuring, manipulation, graphicacy, recording.

Attitudes such as:
Open-mindedness, self-criticism, responsibility, independence of thought, perseverance, co-operation, scepticism, desire to be well informed, confidence, respect, sensitivity, willingness to be involved, tolerance, persuasiveness, questioning, trust.

In the National Curriculum Science document (Department of Education and Science, 1989), there is an extended discussion of skills in science.

A more detailed look at problem-solving skills

Since all our working lives are concerned with the problems of teaching and learning, it would be presumptuous in the extreme to try to solve all 'skills training' in a few paragraphs here. However, teaching for problem-solving must rely on a few assumptions – some that have already been made:

1. That skills like these *can* be taught.
2. It is possible to structure classroom activities to maximize learning.
3. The teaching is 'manageable'; that is, it does not take too much time in preparation or execution in an otherwise busy schedule.

The main assumption, though, is that problems can be analysed in such a way that they can be introduced in succession, in order of difficulty. On the whole, this must be the case — the type of problem a five-year-old might come to terms with is vastly different from the case of a fifteen-year-old. This is not to say that some problems cannot be made applicable across a broad age range: they can. The heart of the matter lies in the bank of problems that are developed over time, and 'the Bank' a teacher might collect is discussed in more detail later.

First, consider, for example, how students learn maths or computer programming from texts. They are often presented with a few pages of material on a particular principle, plus a number of worked-out solutions that illustrate the principle. Then, at the end of that text, a series of problems are presented. The mere fact that they are presented together is a strong clue that they are all somehow related and that the same sub-routines should be used even though the surface features of the problems may differ. The hope is that the students will end up storing a general abstraction which represents a general strategy for solving these types of problem.

If anything, Structured Serendipity means that we have to maximize that hope rather than leaving it to accident. It means that the problems used must be ordered so that they are progressive — they entail slightly different skills each time or the skills are at a slightly different level of difficulty. In this sense it becomes important to follow a sequence:

1. As noted earlier, begin early in school life. Chapter 5 looks at some of the ways problem-solving is used in the curriculum, but the maxim 'start early' holds well. Simple problems with young children set the scene for later work, and this allows the teacher to begin the process of introducing skills.
2. Highlight the skills in each problem. This gives the youngsters a label for some of the activities and so allows the teacher to assist in the carry-over from one task to another.
3. Highlight the context and relevance in each problem. Again, this allows the teacher to frame very similar problems in a slightly different way, to encourage transfer from one situation to another.
4. Reinforce the discussion of skills in the class so that youngsters are able to identify particular activities and reapply them elsewhere.

An example

Let us take an example – the 'separation of materials'. The youngsters are given a problem:

> What we throw out of our homes, and call rubbish, often contains some valuable material. It is important that we can sometimes separate different materials that are mixed together so that some can be recovered and recycled. In this problem you are given a tangle of bits and pieces and must find ways of separating them into different piles in as pure a state as possible, so that they can be used again.

Here the difficulty of the problem lies in the materials used, and the techniques available to the problem-solvers. Paper, metals and other materials can be separated physically by hand, by sieving, or magnetically if there are ferrous and non-ferrous materials present. They can be separated chemically by using a particular solvent (usually water or ethanol) and then recovered from the solution. This can be done, for example, if the mixture contains bits of paper, sand, iron filings, sawdust and salt. The problem can be made much more difficult, though, by considering industrial effluent and trying to separate and recover, say, the immense amount of starch waste that is poured into the environment from a bakery, the high levels of sugar effluent from a sweet factory, or the yeast slurry from a brewery. Each of these materials *can* be separated and recovered, although the problems increase if the separation techniques are meant to cope with a constant flow at high volumes.

Needless to say, these are real industrial problems of the day, and the processes of, for example, recycling paper are issues of current debate.

So, it is not too difficult to design a 'separation problem' that is applicable to a group, for instance at Key Stage 2, 3 or 4. Initially the group may need to be led towards – sometimes directly taught – some of the techniques of separation, the use of the equipment available and the safety issues involved. The same techniques can then be used in a different context ('How can we quickly sort coins of different size and mass?'; 'How can we easily get grass stains out of clothing?') and so on.

The important aspect is that the skills inherent in each problem-solving lesson can be highlighted and discussed, so that they can be known and reintroduced on future occasions. In this sense, problems can be varied in terms of:

- the particular skills and processes that might be involved (physical separation, chemical or biological);
- the 'content area' of the problem (which part of the curriculum it relates to—in science or any other part of schooling);
- the level of difficulty (the number of variables to be considered, the nature of the variables, the complexity of the separation techniques);
- the context in which it might be set (personal, domestic, social, industrial, commercial);
- the time-scale for developing a solution (part of a lesson, a whole lesson, several lessons, etc.);
- the equipment, materials and resources which might be used;
- the nature and level of outcome (purity of the materials recovered, how quickly a solution can be arrived at, etc.).

This analysis is important, and there are no easy short cuts but to work out the best problems with youngsters in the classroom. Some texts use a 'star' rating to indicate the nature of the problem, which range between:

* A straightforward problem, a small number of easily identifiable skills, suitable for Key Stage 1, clear outcomes.
*** Intermediate problem, some identifiable skills but also requiring some improvisation; suitable for Key Stage 3; a variety of outcomes possible.
***** Difficult problem requiring sophisticated techniques; an A-level problem that has a complex set of variables leading to a creative number of outcomes.

A BANK OF PROBLEMS

There is no substitute for building—and categorizing—a bank of problems. Personally, I now have several files of problems, sorted by a code that allows some access according to the sorts of issue already mentioned. So, for example, there are: specifically curriculum problems on, say, force, levers, energy, pressure, electricity and so on; 'stage'-related problems for the National Curriculum Key Stages, post-16, and 'adult' problems; similar problems in different contexts, for example the 'sorting' problem above in domestic and industrial contexts; cross-curricular problems that draw on expertise in several areas of school life; and so on. The problems are collected from many different sources: books on problem-solving; magazines on science and technology; television programmes; conversations with industrialists, colleagues and friends; discussions with pupils as they work. (I suppose it takes a particular outlook on life to be continuously seeking problems!) The problems are graded and sorted as I use them, and as they are tried and tested by a problem-solver. The search, however, is for ways to adapt what is being done, so that there is a need, even at the 'collecting' stage, to:

1. Consider the conceptual space: is the problem doable? Can end-points be visualized (by particular groups of problem-solvers) and contemplated in the circumstances allowed? Are there some possible 'ways' through the problem?
2. Break the problem into parts. Is it really one problem or can a group of connected problems be drawn out of an overall task?
3. Identify the skills. Are there, for instance, skills to be tackled like using a chemical balance, soldering electronic components, preparing a stained microscope slide, using a fretsaw?
4. Look for analogous problems. What is the problem like — is it similar to other problems that I (or others) have solved? What are the similarities, and can they be used in this problem? Can the solution for another problem be translated into a solution for the target problem?
5. Judge whether a series of partial solutions can be developed for the target problem. What counts as a final solution, and can I settle for something else?
6. Think about what hints are readily available from real-world problems. Although the problem at hand is different in some way, can ideas from another context be brought in? Can any rules of thumb be identified in the problem, undertaking what Kahney (1986) calls a Heuristic Search?
7. Consider ways of working backwards or forwards from the goal to the outcome. There are many different preferences as people work and some prefer constantly moving between the start position and the goal, varying the focus of the problem — does the problem allow this or is it very 'linear'?

8. Analyse the problems for likely managerial difficulties, the materials and equipment, the types of room needed, the length of time or 'rules' of competition, the possible disruption to other parts of the school system, and so on.

Banks of problems develop over time and each collector will develop his or her own method of categorizing them — some of the ideas here may help as a check list.

MORE SKILLS

Before leaving the issue of skills, process and attitudes, I want to consider some implications, and amplification, of the skills of problem-solving which are seldom considered. These are sometimes aspects of the skills and processes we take for granted, are integral to problem-solving in action and, I believe, seldom recognized. They include such things as:

* *Observation and evidence as the basis for belief*

A quick example: youngsters were in full flow designing an 'egg transporter' as part of an 'egg-race' activity. One came over to the 'materials station' for an egg and asked if the egg was boiled or raw. I paused for a moment and asked, 'Why? Does it matter?' 'Oh yes', came the reply with utter conviction, 'a boiled egg is heavier than a raw egg'.

The youngsters were building their device based, I guess, on a belief that can only stem from the sensation of robustness: if the egg is more hardy than fragile, it may be tougher and therefore heavier?

Miller (1989) has explored the ways in which evidence in school science is weighed and used and his book provides an interesting critique of what we often take for granted. However, problem-solving (in the way I have been discussing it here) means that problem-solvers actually have to put their own theories into action. Some of this is taken up in the next chapter, but it entails using their conceptualization of the 'way things work'. In many other aspects of school work, youngsters can hide behind the activity and leave their own conceptions in the shadows — problem-solving can bring them to the fore. The skills involved here are difficult to separate, but include the ability to infer, test conjectures through picturing implications, coping with verifiability and insolvability.

- *Use of orders of magnitude, 'guesstimates', use of significant and relevant quantities in measurement*

I recently watched a group of teachers designing and building a 'Hoverloon' – a hovercraft powered by balloon(s), which was required to move forward several metres. The time was short and all failed to produce a working model – they admitted they had little realistic idea of how much weight a balloon could lift, or for how long. In contrast, a group of twelve-year-olds managed this quite easily, and designed several sophisticated versions in roughly the same time allowance. In this sense, problem-solving can make use of, and develop, a range of ancillary skills of quantification.

- *Successive approximations, exploitation of error, feedback and control through iterative processes*

Tinkering with a problem is often regarded as simply 'trial and error', but in fact what might be happening is much more complex and problem-orientated. There may be a constant modification of the situation, a series of small but significant shifts in what is happening. 'Evaluation' and 'redesign' are often part of the problem-solving cycle or process (as discussed above), and by using these words I intended to encompass this set of skills in a large scale and general sense. But these terms fail to capture the constant stream of tiny changes and modifications that take place as the design process is happening. In a sense they deny the absolute notion of 'control of variables' because in a 'rough and ready' solution to a problem there are so many variables that complete control is not possible and changes take place all the time. In this way there can be 'dirty' and 'clean' solutions to a problem – where the problem-solvers have on the one hand opted for a solution 'as good as we can get' (given the time, materials, constraints, etc.), or on the other have tried for the very best possible ideal solution. It is necessary to be able to recognize minor and major fluctuations in the system at hand, or, in the jargon of the trade, understand signal-to-noise ratios;

- *Reductio ad absurdum: pushing ideas to limit*

The initial process of problem-solving, where people contemplate what is possible, what can be done, the extent of the 'problem space', is often called 'brainstorming' or generating ideas. Again, this hides a multiplicity of skills, not least of which is the negotiation of ideas with other people to arrive at a working plan. It is often the most creative phase of problem-solving. The negotiation of ideas (another theme recurring in future chapters) requires the construction (and sometimes demolition) of sets of ideas, and the extension of these into other possibilities. What would happen if . . .? Why can't we . . .? That's ridiculous (absurd, impossible)! Think of it another way . . . These are the kinds of utterances that take place, not at the point of brainstorming when the ideas are presented but at the point of evaluation and selection of ideas. Extending and developing notions, entertaining sometimes fantastic-sounding ideas, involves a set of skills and attitudes seldom counted. But these sorts of skills are invaluable, and would include: being able to see analogies, invoke metaphors; indicate similarities and contrasts, note symmetry and invariance, see equivalences, and congruity; recognize different points of view, be able to change scale, and change the frame of reference; sometimes being able to use anthropomorphism concerning the inanimate;

- *Plurality of approaches*

Similarly, creativity and inventiveness sometimes rely on the ability to hold several seemingly incompatible ideas and approaches in train all at one time. It is the kind of flexibility that rejects a linear approach to a problem, but can set in motion several solutions and can, sometimes, bring these together as an outcome at the end. It is a way of working that is a particular skill in that the problem-solver can cope with (and often relish) the arbitrary rules of the game. Asking a friend for ideas can suggest alternative approaches;

- *Mistrust of the principle of exclusion, or exhaustion; necessary and sufficient conditions, or necessary but not sufficient conditions*

Be both logical and illogical at the same time. Be able to ask the question, 'What if . . .? and 'Why not . . .?'

- *Intellectual elegance, efficiency, taste, style, and judgement*

There has been little mention of overt values in the discussion so far. Values are an important issue and a problem-solver's values will, of course, change the way in which solutions are sought and composed. The National Curriculum documents for Technology (for instance, the NCC's 1989 consultation document) give wide recognition to the discussion of values in design and implementation. For example, as youngsters are working, they are required to understand that artefacts, systems and environments reflect the circumstances and values of particular cultures and communities.

• *Continuity and discontinuity, interpolation and extrapolation*

Some might argue that these are particularly scientific notions, rather than, say, technological ones, or a necessary part of problem-solving. But in many ways they underpin a considerable amount of the discussion of variables (their control or otherwise), since not all variables behave in the same way. This is not the place to discuss the nature of 'nature', whether or not (and how) it is 'chunked' and discrete: there is some discussion of variables in the science Non-Statutory Guidelines (National Curriculum Council, 1989a). In a broad sense, though, these are skills relating to being able to take an overall view of things—to be able to go beyond the information given, or, as we sometimes say, to be able to read between the lines.

Chapter 3

Co-operative Learning, Constructivism and Some Implications for Group Work

This chapter is in several main sections. The first considers three ways of considering activities in the classroom, and focuses on co-operative learning for problem-solving. Next there is a discussion of alternative 'world views' and the impact of constructivism on the curriculum. There then follows a further description of co-operative group work and how the benefits can be harnessed for problem-solving.

INTRODUCTION

I want first to set out three different ways in which classroom work, and therefore problem-solving, can be discussed. In an *individualistic* situation, we recognize that each person in the room has goals and aspirations which are independent of other people in the same room. Everyone is different and their aims and achievements are unrelated to what other people want and do. If we want to go beyond recognizing this as a description of a class and we decide to maximize it, we would structure the curriculum, the management of the class and the mode of teaching and learning so as to emphasize and encourage an independent, individualistic approach.

In a *competitive* situation, each person's work is very much related to what those around are doing, although the relationship is one of trying to establish superiority (or being reconciled to inferiority) in a perceived or real ranking system. In this sense, in a strictly competitive situation, if one person or group manages to attain the goals set, it means that others will have failed to meet the goal in some may (win the prize, achieve first place, etc.). To teach for this sort of approach is, of course, to emphasize the element of competition and to structure the classroom and school ethos accordingly.

In a *co-operative* situation, individuals' goals are positively linked with those of others — when one person achieves the target it means that all those with whom he or she is linked will also have achieved their goal. Co-operative learning is more difficult to establish because it relies on the temperaments, common goals, attitudes, skills, ideas, etc. of several people, working in accord and trying to achieve a positive result. Again, to establish this sort of working ethos in classrooms means that we must seek to emphasize the benefits and rewards of co-operative work, structure the learning environment to facilitate this and teach and develop social skills alongside other curricular skills.

These are not the only three ways of talking about classrooms but they serve my needs here in discussing problem-solving. Needless to say, if we were to look at any one classroom, we would probably find all three modes present at the same time. Some individuals are very independent, preferring to work on their own: they may work exceedingly well that way, developing their own ideas and projects. Others relish competition, are forever watching what others are doing so that they can gain an advantage and 'better' them, and derive immense pride and satisfaction from having beaten their rivals, neighbours or friends. Yet others will enjoy working together, commonly in friendship groups; they will feed from and into the group task, support others and take comfort from a group achievement.

It is also possible that any one individual can move between modes in different circumstances, being individualistic when it suits, highly competitive when the opportunity arises and working well within a co-operative task at other times. Similarly, different teachers will teach with these different ways of working in mind, so that they will sometimes emphasize individual work, sometimes sponsor competition, and often look for youngsters to work together co-operatively.

There is no great consensus in the research literature as to which mode is most successful. The review of literature by Johnson *et al.* (1979) concluded that it depends largely on the learning to be done — different modes suit different tasks for different people at different times. Of particular interest here, though, is the general agreement that co-operative working is very important for problem solving — it resulted in higher achievement than the other modes where problem-solving is concerned. For example, Johnson *et al.* (1979) say:

> Since exchanging information may facilitate the solving of [these] complex tasks, these findings are congruent with the previous research that has found, [for] tasks requiring interdependence among students, or involving problem solving and conceptual learning, [that] a cooperative goal structure is more facilitative of achievement than is an individualistic or competitive one.

The 'previous research' they refer to here is, in part, some of their own (Johnson *et al.*, 1978), where they say that co-operative learning also promotes positive attitudes towards peers, higher self-esteem, more positive attitudes towards teachers and fellow co-operators, more self-discipline and higher daily achievements. These are heady claims and if we felt confident they would apply at all times and in all circumstances there would be an overnight rush to 'co-operative learning' techniques.

In schools we are probably somewhat cautions and would prefer to 'mix and match' ways of working to suit different classes at different times. In mixing, it is probable that teachers will want to capitalize on the classroom benefits of each one of the three modes. We want youngsters to develop their independence and individual approaches to life — in fact is often very difficult to do otherwise. There is a place for the challenge that comes from competition and 'the test', 'the race' or 'the finals' can be humorous, exciting and very popular. And co-operative learning can have many of the benefits already noted. So, in problem-solving, problems can sometimes best be tackled individually, sometimes as a challenge (as in 'egg-race' problem-solving) and sometimes as a group endeavour.

My central points here, though, are that:

- problem-solving can greatly benefit from co-operative working;
- co-operative learning itself can greatly benefit from tackling problem-solving tasks;
- we need to work at developing co-operative learning — it does not necessarily happen automatically — and a useful way forward is to consider team tasks;
- 'individualism' and co-operative learning can sometimes seem at odds with each other — a major aspect of co-operative learning is the negotiation of the 'world views' of individuals.

But before we can go any further with group work and problem-solving, I need to discuss what I mean in the last point, by people's 'world views'.

WORLD VIEWS

In the mid-1970s a considerable body of science education research focused on what have been called alternative conceptions, alternative frameworks, misconceptions, preconceptions, children's science, youngsters' world views and so on. Although numerous papers were produced before that time, the research developed momentum in about 1978, with the publication of a seminal article by Ros Driver and Jack Easley, who were the first to coin the phrase 'alternative frameworks' (Driver and Easley, 1978). These authors examined the research in science which explored what understandings, ideas and views learners *do* have, rather than those they do not have, things they cannot do, or the errors they make.

Learners' 'frameworks of understanding', or 'world views', are important because they help individuals to shape new information and experiences. We come to understand things in terms of what we already understand; if we cannot lock new ideas into the ideas we have already generated, then new experiences become somewhat meaningless.

In the last decade or so, books, papers, articles, reports, conferences, proceedings, whole editions of journals, and entire theses and dissertations have been devoted to discussing pupils' world views. A bibliography being compiled through the Children's Learning in Science Project and the Secondary Science Curriculum Review (Driver *et al.*, 1990) has several hundred items listed. The interested reader can find many examples of this work detailed in Pfundt and Duit (1988) and discussed in Driver *et al.* (1985), Osborne and Freyberg (1985), Fensham (1988), White (1988) and Adey *et al.* (1989).

Much of this research has provided a fairly extensive catalogue of the content of youngsters' ideas in science. It is clear that school pupils have a number of unorthodox ideas about a wide range of topics; that these ideas can remain intact in the face of normal everyday teaching; that they can shape how learners make sense of new data and information, and that they can even persist in the face of counter-argument and evidence to the contrary.

The research so far has been referred to as 'the butterfly hunt', or 'stamp collecting': the data collecting stage which sometimes invites more questions than can be answered. How do alternative frameworks and individual world views develop? Are they really coherent frameworks of ideas or a hotch-potch of associations and impressions? Which are the best methods of exploring them in classrooms? Are there as many ideas on a topic as there are learners in the class, or is there a restricted number for each topic area? And, most importantly, what do we *do* once we know about them – can they be changed and, if so, how best can we organize that?

A start has been made in providing answers. Conceptions develop as individuals respond to the myriad of everyday influences and experiences around them. One might wonder why, for example, youngsters find it difficult to believe that a dusty old book lying on a shelf has energy. Energy, they would argue, is to do with movement, activity, liveliness, living. Most people will have seen the advertisement for electricity showing a newborn baby in an incubator over the caption 'Energy for life', or have watched the chocolate advert on television which suggests that one bar gives you all the energy you need to 'work, rest and play'. Quite clearly, teachers are not the only source of learning experiences, and youngsters' 'life-world knowledge', as Joan Solomon (1985) describes it, is reinforced by many powerful images.

SOME EXAMPLES

Whether about force (Terry *et al.*, 1985), energy (Solomon, 1985; Brook and Wells, 1988), heat (Clough and Driver, 1985), electricity (Shipstone, 1988), or 'animals', 'living', 'nutrition', 'light', 'radioactivity' and so on, there is ample evidence that young people do generate their own theories and use these quite happily as they explain phenomena in the world. In this sense they act as young scientists. Nor are alternative 'world views' the sole prerogative of youngsters: Furnham (1988) has documented such ideas in many walks of adult life; Summers and Kruger *et al.* (1989) have done so for teachers of science in schools.

It is worth repeating that the important issue is that such ideas shape how learners make sense of new data and information; that these 'world views' can remain intact in the face of normal everyday teaching, and can even persist in the face of powerful counter-argument and counter-evidence.

Example 1

David, 14 years old, discusses the forces on a golf ball in flight through the air. Is there, he is asked, a force on the golf ball in the direction of flight? 'Of course', comes the reply, 'I've been hit by a golf ball and it hurts! If you stuck your head in the way and it hit you, you'd feel a force there all right.'

From the scientist's point of view, David is not correct. There is no force in the direction of motion, there is only the force of gravity acting vertically downwards and the friction from the air acting in a direction opposite to the motion.

David's response is very similar to that of many other people (Watts, 1983). He sees forces as quite tangible and obvious from their effects. He goes on to say that if there were *not* a force in the direction of motion then the ball would have no reason to go on, no 'motive power' and would therefore stop.

David: 'It must have a force driving it forward. If it didn't it would stop . . . like a car if you take your foot off the accelerator.'

For many people the construction that 'motion means a force' is highly resistant to change. So much so that many physics students cannot cope with basic problems in physics where the direction of motion does not coincide with the direction of the net force. In this case, like many other people, they have used daily experiences to build models of how the world works and which allow them to make sense of the world they know. That this does not always comply with the way that scientists describe the world is a problem for science teachers.

Example 2

Lou, 13 years old, was asked to predict and compare the times taken for one-inch cubes of plastic and aluminium to fall about two metres. He answered that the heavier aluminium cube would hit the ground first (Gunstone and Watts, 1985). He supported his prediction by claiming to have dropped different weights off a bridge and to have seen the heavier one reach the ground first. When the two cubes were dropped in the laboratory, he claimed that the aluminium one actually struck before the plastic one. He would not relinquish this idea despite the efforts of the teacher to show that they do arrive at the same time.

Example 3

Cathy is 14 years old and discussing aspect of heat. She develops a model of the earth's atmosphere where the temperature gradient is such that temperature increases with distance from the earth's surface. She begins by making the commonplace comment that 'heat rises'. What does she think happens as the distance from the ground increases? 'It gets hotter and hotter', she responds. The next question sets out to explore this further, and asks what happens at altitude, at the upper reaches of the atmosphere.

Cathy: 'It gets very, very hot. That's why things burn up when they come into the atmosphere. That's why that space shuttle needs those heat-resistant tiles.'

Example 4

During a similar session, Colin, age 15, develops a different model in which the gradient of atmospheric pressure increases with distance. This increasing air pressure does have a finite end – at the edge of the atmosphere where Colin postulates a kind of barrier before space is reached. There is a 'layer' which represents an invisible shield around the earth, he suggests. This atmospheric pressure model explains why a toy balloon bursts as it rises – it implodes owing to the increasing pressure.

Both Cathy and Colin are able to retain their models intact in the face of further questioning (Watts, 1983). For example, Cathy was asked how she would explain, in terms of her model of heat, why there is snow on very high mountains. After a puzzled moment she said: 'No, I'm not sure. But I do know it is hot up there . . . my friend went skiing at Christmas and she got sunburned.'

These examples have all come from physics but it is not difficult to show that similar sorts of models, ideas and conceptions occur in all other parts of science.

LEARNING AS CONCEPTUAL CHANGE

In some respects, what teachers do with learners' alternative frameworks like these is a matter of philosophy and style. Some will want to ignore them, work for 'the exam' and trust they will go away in good time. Some will want to spend lessons challenging the ideas so that students can come to appreciate the 'physics way'. This can quite clearly be much more difficult. Moreover, the methods of achieving this are uncertain, unproven, time-consuming and exhausting. To do *something* for learners' concepts, however, stems from a view that learning entails conceptual change: it is only by reflecting, exploring, testing, amending and revising our current concepts to meet new circumstances and experiences that we undertake meaningful learning. This is an important issue then, as far as problem-solving is concerned.

To begin to use or tackle youngsters' frameworks of ideas seriously, we need to know how widespread and stubbornly rooted they are. It is not just advertising and television, but a host of everyday experiences and physical sensations which go to support intuitive and 'commonsense' ideas. Alternative conceptions appear at all levels of schooling up to physics A-level, and have been reported at graduate and postgraduate level. We must take this as an indication that they are fairly resistant to change.

Figure 3.1 is one I have used before (Watts, 1988) in an attempt to illustrate some of the factors. Some conceptions are shared by a large number of people, and so the probability of finding that conception present in the responses from members of a class must be high. Other conceptions are the product of particular experiences and ways of thinking, and so might be specific only to a small number of individuals. Some conceptions are easily changed while others must be deep-seated and charged with significance, making them difficult to alter.

How we place conceptions in this matrix might influence our choice of strategies for teaching. For example, conceptions in quadrant A could be dealt with quite quickly with the whole class. An instance might be of students who have a 'clashing current' model of electric circuits: who suggest that current comes out in opposite directions from the ends of the battery and clashes in the bulb to produce light. In talking to a group, the model might be attributed to 'pupils I taught last year' and explored in terms of bulbs in series and in

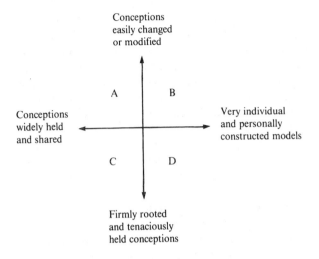

Figure 3.1 A conceptual matrix. Source: Watts (1988).

parallel to show how the model is severely limited.

Conceptions in quadrant B are more difficult to unearth and would probably be apparent in discussion groups, individual answers to questions and homeworks. They would probably be best tackled individually, too.

More worrisome are conceptions in quadrant C. These have been the subject of most of the research into conceptual change. An example might be the motion of a projectile—a golf ball, for example—through the air. Large numbers of youngsters will argue as David did in Example 1 above, contrary to classical physics, that there is a force in the direction of motion. The force is needed to account for the object's movement and, if there were no force, it is said, then the object would stop immediately. The arguments are deep-seated and reinforced by commonsense interpretations of events in everyday life.

One possible approach is to help learners develop shared models of what they think is happening, and then spend time working through them in detail. Nussbaum and Novick (1982), in their article 'Brainstorming in the classroom', give some indication of how this might work. In their example, teachers invited the class to explore various models of the nature of gases and to 'test the models to destruction'. This resulted in some change towards a 'particulate nature of gases' model. Other researchers have sought ways of easing the transition from personal construction to scientific model by means of strategic stepping-stones or (in the jargon of the trade) through bridging exercises. Jim Minstrell's 'The at-rest conditions of a body' (Minstrell, 1982) is an example of this way of working. The Children's Learning in Science Project has been exploring many ways in which conceptions can be exposed, explored and exploited within classrooms. This work is now becoming available as classroom packs (Children's Learning in Science, 1987).

Finally, conceptions in quadrant D are the most difficult to contend with. For instance, a youngster might develop very interesting and creative models about light (Watts, 1985). Such conceptions are usually the most interesting in that they allow some window upon the ways in which conceptions develop. It may well be beyond the scope and resources of most classroom teachers, though, to enable conceptual change if the conceptions are both fairly idiosyncratic and tenaciously held.

THE NATIONAL CURRICULUM AGAIN

In their proposals to the Secretary of State, the Science Working Group (Department of Education and Science, 1988) adopted a very clear 'child-centred' perspective. The child, they said, is the agent of his or her own learning in science. Children's learning in science is linked by analogy to scientists' advancement of ideas, hypotheses and principles when faced with new phenomena. Their prior knowledge and initial theorizing are therefore important as part of the process of reaching a scientific understanding of the world around them.

In many respects this way of working lies within a constructivist perspective. The Science Working Group's ideas are brave ones because a 'learner-centred' approach does not have universal appeal (certainly not in practice) and has not always been in favour with curriculum planners. The tendency in the past has been to find (possibly) a 'child-centred' approach in primary schools and a much more instructional, examination-orientated mode in secondary schools. While some of the brave words were lost by the time the curriculum arrived at the statute books, there are still some encouraging signs in the final version of the National Curriculum 'Document' (Department of Education and Science, 1989). For instance, there it indicates (among other things) that pupils should be encouraged to develop their understanding of science through explorations which:

- are set within their everyday experiences and which at different times:
- require the deployment of previously encountered concepts and investigative skills to solve practical problems;
- encourage pupils to articulate their own ideas and work independently or contribute to group efforts;
- promote invention and creativity;
- require pupils to generate theoretical models and test them by investigation;
- enable pupils to distinguish between claims and arguments based on scientific considerations and those which are not.

Moreover, other aspects of the Working Party's original considerations survive in the Non-Statutory Guidelines produced by the National Curriculum Council (1989a). One might assume that behind these sorts of statements lies a particular view of the process of learning; few curriculum statements in the past, for instance, have required pupils to generate and test their *own* theories and debate the validity of evidence. But all this leads now to a discussion of constructivism.

ONE VIEW OF CONSTRUCTIVISM

Constructivism is an umbrella for a range of theories — and theorists — who share common points of view. Mahoney (1988), for instance, notes that:

> Constructivism refers to a family of theories that share the assertion that human knowledge and experience entail the (pro)active participation of the individual.

Here I want to focus on just one member of the family: George Kelly's Theory of Personal Constructs (Kelly, 1955). I have discussed the impact of Kelly's work on education elsewhere (Pope and Watts, 1988; Watts and Pope, 1989). In his theory, Kelly takes his root metaphor as 'man the scientist'. He invites us to suppose that, in the course of their everyday lives, everyday people act like everyday scientists:

> might not the individual man, each in his own personal way, assume more of the stature of a scientist, ever seeking to predict and control the course of events with which he is involved? Would he not have his theories, test his hypotheses, and weigh his experimental evidence? And if so, might not the differences between the personal viewpoints of different men correspond to the differences between theoretical points of view of different scientists?

The essence of Kelly's ideas is that each person erects for himself or herself a model of the world that enables him/her to chart a course of behaviour within it. Like a scientist's model, this model is subject to change over time since constructions of reality are constantly being tested and modified to allow a better working model to be erected. And 'better' or 'worse' here means how well the model serves people in predicting and sorting out what is happening as they go about their daily business. As Johnson-Laird (1983) points out:

> Human beings . . . do not apprehend the world directly; they possess only an internal representation of it, because perception is the construction of a model of the world. They are unable to compare this perceptual representation directly with the world – it IS their world.

Kelly's theory emphasizes 'anticipation'. People who anticipate events successfully have built a coherent construct system. This system can account for previous experiences, interpret present circumstances, shape forecasts of approaching eventualities and help assess the accuracy of past predictions. Kelly lays great stress on the uniqueness of each person's construct system; a key assumption within his theory is the 'individuality corollary': 'Persons differ from each other in their constructions of events.' People are restlessly proactive – they set about interpreting their own world, they are not just passive recipients of someone else's knowledge. Kelly also sets great store by individuals' trying to make clear their ideas to themselves and to others with whom they interact. In teaching, this is important on two counts:

- it allows the teacher to have some understanding of the personal models that the learners have as they impose meaning on the world – to learn something about the learner;
- in the process of communicating ideas, the learner has an opportunity to clarify thoughts so that he or she can recognize how they might be changed (if at all) – for the learner to think about his/her own thinking.

The theory of Personal Constructs is not a suggestion that people actually are scientists, simply that viewing people in their 'science-like aspects' can illuminate human behaviour.

Constructivism and the curriculum

Kelly's is not the only constructivist theory. The early Piaget, for instance, was very constructivist (before, some say, he later went too 'structuralist'), and latter-day constructivism has many adherents. Driver (1988) lists six features of a constructivist perspective as it impacts on schooling:

- Learners are not viewed as passive but are seen as purposive and ultimately responsible for their own learning. They bring their prior conceptions to learning situations.
- Learning is considered to involve an active process on the part of the learner. It involves the construction of meaning and often takes place through interpersonal negotiation.
- Knowledge is not 'out there' but is personally and socially constructed; its status is problematic. It may be evaluated by the individual in terms of the extent to which it fits with their experience and is coherent with other aspects of their knowledge.
- Teachers also bring their prior conceptions to learning situations not only in terms of their subject knowledge but also their views of teaching and learning. These can influence their ways of interacting in the classroom.
- Teaching is not the transmission of knowledge but involves the organization of the situations in the classroom and the design of tasks in a way which promotes scientific learning.
- The curriculum is not that which is to be learned, but a programme of learning tasks, materials and resources from which students construct their knowledge.

This kind of approach generates a different view of what teaching is and how it might be carried out in the classroom. It is consistent with the National Curriculum Science Working Party's point when they say:

> The ideas of young children can be essentially scientific in so far as they fit the available evidence, even though they will tend to be limited to concrete observable features and will also be a long way short of formal theories. Inevitably children's ideas will change as their experience widens. . . . There is an essential role for the teacher as enabler in this process: the teacher may interact with the pupil, raise questions, build in appropriate challenges and experiences, and offer new ways of thinking.

Within any one topic area students might display a range of understandings which are the consequences of their adroit personal interpretations of phenomena. Constructivism would say that this is a fundamental feature of the act of human learning, a consequence of individual development within a complex social and linguistic context, and one that cannot be eradicated.

In this sense, the teacher's job becomes that of:

- encouraging the pupil to share and eventually own the purpose for the lessons or activity;
- developing learning experiences that allow pupils to take responsibility for the design, process and outcomes of the investigation;
- valuing pupils' hypotheses and conclusions and generating discussion of the scientific description of what has been taking place in the activity.

This is a difficult task. As Osborne and Freyberg (1985) say:

> Effective implementation of [these] ideas . . . requires active teaching by a teacher who clearly appreciates children's ideas, the scientific view to be encouraged, the types of activities which might achieve conceptual change and the associated interactive teaching sequences which need to be adopted.

This is, we need to provide more opportunities for pupils to talk about what they are doing, to become aware of their own ideas and those of their peers, and to modify their own ideas where necessary. It is not a task or job description that is familiar to many science teachers — and it is certainly not easy:

> How can teachers carry out what they believe to be their responsibilities when these include control of pupils' learning and encouraging

pupils actively to formulate knowledge? In one direction lies control so strong that school knowledge remains alien to the learner (whether he [or she] rejects it or goes along with it); in the other direction lies a withdrawal of guidance, so that learners never need to grapple with alternative ways of thinking. The teacher has to find his [or her] way between the two.

Barnes (1976)

Constructivism and problem-solving

At first sight there may seem to be a conflict between the sorts of arguments I have been pursuing so far. First I have been extolling the virtues of problem-solving as a way of working in the classroom. In this chapter I have been focusing on co-operative learning as a boon to problem-solving, but have now spent some while detailing constructivism, which seems to put a premium on individualism. From what has been said above, a constructivist perspective highlights a child-centred approach, one which seems more individualistic and respects people's ideas for their own sake, eschews normative judgements, and does not mention competition, let alone co-operation.

However, it is important to appreciate that the construction of frameworks, models and world views does not happen in a social vacuum – other people are vital at each point in the construction. One clear way in which individuals develop their ideas, test them and evaluate the outcomes is with other people. Friends, colleagues and others trigger ideas – through personal interaction, books, television, films, etc. – and we then proceed to bounce these off people around us to see how well they work, what kind of reception they receive. There are some people who would argue that life and human development could not be any other way: we are what we are because of the society in which we live – the 'individual–society' dualism is outmoded. 'The individual as a concept', say Henriques *et al.* (1984), 'could not exist without its opposite number, society'. Indeed, as individuals we are the product of the discourses which have developed over time.

While my own preference in psychology falls a little short of the extremes, I can clearly see the point in such statements: as individuals, our conceptions, language, values, mores and attitudes are moulded and honed by the society which we inhabit. For youngsters at school that society is made up of home, play, school, television, books, magazines, etc. — and all the interpersonal space in between.

Learning is inextricably linked with communication, and by 'communication' is meant a sharing or exchange of ideas (see Bentley and Watts, 1990). This is essentially a two-way (or multi-way) process. That is, communication requires some response from the people at the other end of the communiqué; communication is not a one-way transfer. To have someone communicate *at* you is not communication at all. Hence the truth in the kind of expression 'I can't communicate with Chris, it's like talking to a brick wall'.

What this boils down to is that both learning and communicating are essentially group activities. The strong position adopted elsewhere (Bentley and Watts, 1990) is that *all* learning takes place through group communication. That is, individual acts are subservient to the group's requirements and not the other way round. Within this is the recognition of the paradox at the heart of all schooling — as teachers we teach groups but assess individuals. More of this later.

GROUP WORK

A system of co-operative group working and sharing ideas in problem-solving has many advantages:

- it removes much of the personal pressure which some pupils might feel when first presented with a problem;
- the contribution of individuals, each with their own strengths, can allow a team to work quickly and logically towards a solution;
- working in small groups gives less-confident pupils the opportunity to take part;
- it is a method of working which is well established in primary schools and may go some way to easing the transition of pupils from primary school to secondary schools;
- the work of individual groups can be tailored to fit the abilities of each particular group;
- by questioning and discussing each other's ideas the pupils can sort out a clearer picture of the problem and the steps needed to solve it.

It is this final point that is important and is discussed more fully in Chapter 4. Solutions to problems do not come out of 'thin air';

the seeds to the solution lie in what youngsters already know, in their 'prior knowledge'. There need not be one right answer or correct solution to the problem; they can be open to a variety of outcomes. This means that problem-solvers are free; they are encouraged to develop their own ideas. It is a rich opportunity for individuals to make explicit, explore and debate their ideas of how things work.

All in all, then, group problem-solving has a lot going for it. But what factors increase the productivity of group learning? To what extent does progress depend upon the 'learning environment'; the negotiation of 'group rules'; the direct teaching of group learning skills? Slavin (1978) has looked at some of the factors that influence group work, for example:

- the level of individual responsibility for group members instead of group outcomes;
- the nature of any group reward system;
- the extent of a structured schedule of activities tied to a team programme.

He makes the point that it is possible to retain some of the best features of co-operative learning alongside some of the elements of competitiveness, by developing 'teams'. In this system, pupils' rewards and motivation depend on the performance of a group, which can vary in size from a 'pairing' to the entire class. Each member's performance helps others meet their goals:

> As a result, students encourage one another to do well, and express strong norms in favour of performance that moves the team towards success.

However, he adds two caveats to this system: mutual help and encouragement only happen to the extent that individuals are responsible for their own work. In a group that is judged simply by the corporate product (a single report or project), there may be little point in encouraging low performers to do their best, as it may be easier for the more able students to do the work themselves than to motivate others to contribute.

However, to set against that, the effects of co-operative working on interpersonal relationships are more clear than the effects on performance. Slavin (1978) says:

> An effect almost invariably found in research on cooperation is an increase in such variables as group members' mutual attraction

and feelings of being liked. This outcome is important in all schools, but particularly in integrated schools, where many studies have shown that cooperative, multi-racial teams lead to cross-racial friendship.

There are also some implications of using this co-operative group approach; for example:

- it needs a system of recording the progress of each group;
- it needs a high level of organization such that there is always material available for each group's needs;
- it needs determination on the part of the teacher to get round and talk to each group at some point in the lesson;
- the whole class needs to be brought together regularly to share ideas and to discuss the work covered.

BEGINNING PROBLEM-SOLVING WORK IN SCHOOL

The ideal size of group, according to Rowlands (1987), is three, although there are advantages in other group sizes (as discussed, for example, in Bentley and Watts, 1990). Groups of two are sometimes called dyads or pairings, and have their own particular advantages and disadvantages. For example, there is a considerable volume of work on dyads in terms of 'peer tutoring' where the work is structured so that pupils can learn directly from one another. Sharan (1980) for instance has studied dyads as compared to larger teams and sees both as having benefits and drawbacks—depending on what the teacher wants to achieve in the class. Kutnik and Thomas (1989) have argued that pairs or dyads are particularly effective where conceptual development is concerned. In some cases it is possible to write problem briefs with two pupils in mind, as the following examples show:

Problem 1: Brenda and Po Chui

Brenda and Po Chui had just come back from a day trip to Calais on a hovercraft. They were arguing about the way the vehicle was able to hover and travel. Brenda bet she could make a balloon-powered hovercraft which would beat anything that Po Chui could make. They agreed they would only use materials they could get from school and that the craft must be supported and driven by the air from the balloon—they weren't allowed to push it at the start.

1. What practical problems do you have to sort out first?
2. What would be a fair test of the best Hover-loon?
3. What apparatus and materials will you need?
4. Draw your plans before you start and make notes about any changes you try as you do them – you won't remember later!
5. If you had more time or could start again, what would you do in order to make your Hover-loon go better or further?

Problem 2: Sharmi and Ceris

Sharmi and Ceris were talking about clocks. They wanted to work together to make a timing device that could do two sets of timings: it could accurately signal when twenty seconds had elapsed and stop when a minute was up. They could only use the materials that they could find in the classroom, although they had found a wooden stand with three holes in it. How would you make the clock?

1. What practical problems do you have to sort out first?
2. What would be a fair test of the timer?
3. What apparatus and materials will you need?
4. Draw your plans before you start and make notes about any changes you try as you do them – you won't remember later!
5. If you had longer to work or could start again, what would you do in order to make your timer more accurate or more reliable?

Problem 3: Eddie and Carmelene

Eddie and Carmelene have spent the day with a small local company that makes toys and games. One game needs a thirty-second delay device. The production team say that it has to be started by a marble and that the end of the thirty seconds is signalled by a marble being ejected. The team says that there is further money available for development if they get a good idea. Eddie and Carmelene had only the materials they could find around them, plus a few marbles from home. How would you make a delay device?

1. What practical problems do you have to sort out first?
2. What would be a fair test of the delay device?
3. What apparatus and materials will you need?
4. Draw your plans before you start and make notes about any changes you try as you do them – you won't remember later!

5. If you had longer to work or could start again, what would you do in order to make your device more accurate or more reliable? Could you make one that produced a much longer delay?

Problem-solving, then, can be easily designed for, and accomplished in, pairs, but in the rest of this chapter I will use the word 'group' to mean more than two but usually no greater than six. Whatever the case, it is important that, as far as possible, the teacher chooses the group, or team, and does not allow youngsters to work together simply on the basis of friendship patterns. The number in each group is usually dictated by the number of pupils in the whole class — and by the teacher's judgement of how many different tasks can be countenanced in the room at the same time. So, with thirty in the class, the decision may be six groups of five or five groups of six, rather than, say, ten groups of three.

For the teacher with no tradition of doing problem-solving there is no other way than to 'try it and see'. It is best to design the teams on a fairly random basis, making sure that groups have a reasonable spread of abilities, gender and backgrounds, and that the random selection has not put sworn enemies in the same group. In secondary school, different teachers have different ways of first attempting problem-solving:

- using an (easy to get at) tutor group
- using a trusted class
- drawing teams from the Science Club.

One way to begin is to enter a local or national competition — there are now several which use an 'egg-race' format. Because such events are usually held annually, there is some time to arrange entries and for teams to practise before the event.

Schools can often enter several teams (in different age groups) and there are a number of ways in which this has been organized by schools in the past. In the ESSO Challenge (see Surrey Satro, 1989), for example, each school can involve as many students as it likes, but must eventually select one team for each of the three age groups to go forward from the school to an area final. A team consists of six members of the same age.

Choosing the teams — and finding the one to go forward to represent the school — can be tackled in a number of ways. For example, if it is announced to the whole school that teams are invited to participate in the event, then it might be that teams must gather themselves together and bring the organizer their list of names (and named reserves) by a certain deadline. In some cases schools have had a big turnout of teams and have run a 'mini-event' as a way of selecting teams for the area final.

Where a science club or 'egg-race club' exists then this has sometimes been used for the process of team selection. The teacher selecting the teams (rather than allowing the teams to select themselves) needs to look at several points:

- The kind of roles that youngsters can play: it is no good having a team full of 'lateral thinkers'; it also needs some 'doers', 'organizers' and 'convergent thinkers', and people who can change role too.
- Individuals who can both work alone and work in a team: team members sometimes need to take responsibility for just one part of the problem and then bring that back to fit in with what everyone else has been doing.
- Youngsters who 'get on' with each other: there are no hard-and-fast rules here — the 'chemistry' of groups is not an exact science. The best thing to say is that teachers know better than anyone what friendship patterns exist, and how best to use this effectively.

There is no doubt that the more practice they get the better pupils will work together. Of course there are many other models of how one might introduce problem-solving, and some of these are discussed in Chapter 5.

Whether pupils continue to work in the same groups must be based on:

- how well they work together in the first instance;
- the nature of the task;
- the duration of the task.

For example, a group of six may break up into smaller groups in order to share out the work, and then come together again as the tasks near completion. If the problems to be solved are short and there are several to be tackled in a kind of 'circus' of events, it may be best to leave groups together as they work through the activities. On the other hand, if there are to be different problems to be solved over several weeks of work, it may be best to choose different teams each time. In Bentley and Watts (1990) we discuss some of the many different ways of sorting groups and the benefits to be derived from changing teams regularly.

The final points to be made in this chapter are similar to the points made about transfer of learning: that youngsters need to be taught how to work in groups and that teaching needs to be overt. Burden *et al.* (1988), for instance, indicate that collaborative group work has benefits for even the youngest of children and that all groups benefit from feedback about their work as a group and their group skills. Group skills include being able to take turns in such activities as talking, listening, doing ('You go first, then I'm next'); being able to organize themselves and keep the activity going ('One more thing to do'); support each other ('Go on, try! It doesn't matter if it doesn't work'); suggesting alternatives ('What about these?'); explaining ('That goes there because it's little'); commenting ('Looks like we've done it wrong again') and finishing ('We're finished, it's done!).

Feedback can be given in terms of how well the group managed these sorts of skill and a discussion of some of the weaker points, allowing the group to suggest remedies for the next time they work together or for when each of the individuals works in another group.

Chapter 4

Transferring Learning, Owning the Problems

This chapter considers some of the aspects of the transfer of learning in creativity in design and problem-solving, and looks to see whether and how it is possible to teach transfer in the classroom. It also looks at the ownership of problems in school problem-solving. The first part of the chapter pursues the following line of discussion: problem-solving relies upon the transfer of learning, often experiential learning, which is brought to bear upon a novel situation or activity. We want to enhance 'appropriate' transfer and we need to think about class-room implications of this. There follows the question: to what extent can personal ownership of ideas be achieved? Can the 'act of contributing' to co-operative learning and the resultant process of negotiation be taught? Can a *group* generate ideas – or does the development of ideas depend on the status of the individuals in the group?

LEARNING AND UNDERSTANDING

Problem-solving is different from other activities in the classroom because the pupils themselves take over some of the responsibility for organizing what they are learning. It is possible to set out a number of ways in which pupils learn in science and technology as they are working; for instance, by:

- practising skills they have already learned – like separation techniques, cutting and drilling, construction by triangulation, or weighing and measuring;

- practising some of the processes they already know, like forming hypotheses, testing ideas or devising fair tests;
- using concepts and understandings they already have, like the mechanics of levers, properties of materials, hydraulic pressure or force and friction;
- learning new ideas as they research aspects of the problem in books, texts, videos, etc. or from the teacher or other adults at hand;
- learning new ideas and skills from other members of the group as they introduce these to the problem and share them within the team;
- developing positive attitudes so that, for example, they might appreciate that learning and doing can be fun, accept other people's opinions, learn how to work in a team, leading and co-operating;
- increasing their abilities to communicate so that, for instance, they might learn how to listen better, know how and when to make a telling contribution, write with a particular audience in mind, report the group's activities to the whole class, write to a local business and so on.

The important part about learning is that it happens all the time, with or without a teacher present. We often make the mistake of thinking that learning can only happen in classrooms, or that what happens in classrooms ensures that meaningful learning takes place. Neither is true, of course, and not all learning is what we would consider to be 'good'. People learn 'bad' habits: learn to be mean, rude, prejudiced, violent, disruptive and so on. The best we can say is that, as teachers, we intervene in the learning process and try to manage the transfer of *desirable* learning from one context to another.

However, as the discussion of constructivism in Chapter 3 noted, people are very different and, as a matter of human course, will interpret circumstances in their own way so that the construction of a set of events, or of a learning situation, is not something that can be guaranteed. Learning, that is, means that different people will transfer different constructions from one set of circumstances to another. As McKeachie (1987) says:

> Transfer is paradoxical. When we want it, we do not get it. Yet it occurs all the time. . . . We never use learning in exactly the same

situation in which we have learned it. Even in the laboratory, recall is in a different context than that in which the original learning occurred, for neither the situation nor the learner can be held constant.

That is, transfer is selective — learners, or problem-solvers, *choose* which aspects of one context they will carry over to another, although they may not do this consciously. When confronted by a new situation they will want to construe this in terms of what they already know and understand. There will be some feature of the new situation that will lock into a scheme the learner has already constructed:

'I think this is probably a case of . . .'
'It seems a bit like . . .'
'Well, I think we're talking here about . . .'

TEACHING FOR TRANSFER

If transfer is selective and depends upon individual personal constructions, is it possible to teach for transfer? In my view the answer is yes, at two levels. The first level is the general level, and this entails a brief discussion of 'metacognition'. The second is at the very specific level and depends on the analysis of the contexts and problems involved.

Metacognition

How well, or otherwise, individuals manage to transfer appropriate (or desirable) learning would seem to depend on three things:

- cognitive factors — 'quick-wittedness'; the ability to recall; versatile thinking skills; imagination; learning style;
- motivational factors — self-esteem; expectations; 'learned helplessness'; personal attitudes; self-direction; emotional state;
- social factors — peer evaluation; a relaxed, non-threatening environment; competition, etc.

Metacognition can be defined as attempts to get a learner to think actively about his or her own learning and consciously develop a range of learning styles. Metacognition deals with the extent to which people are aware of their own state, in particular their own cognition and learning. The general feeling is that the more that learners can become aware of their own learning, then the more control they have and the greater the learning that can take place.

In science education there have been a number of studies that have explored metacognition and 'meta-learning'. Novak (1985), for instance, discusses his work with undergraduates in terms of Ausubel's theory of meaningful learning. His main tool has been concept mapping where, essentially, students are asked to draw 'spider diagrams' of the ideas and links between ideas in a particular situation. They are asked to think about their diagrams and identify concepts, the relationships between concepts, and the way in which these have been arranged on their map. In this way, they are being asked to 'think about their thinking'. Similarly, Strike and Posner (1985) have developed their ideas of conceptual change in terms of meaningful learning. They say that before new ideas can be considered in their fullest, so that an individual's conceptions can change, the new ideas must be intelligible, plausible and fruitful. That is, they must make some sense, have some point to them and appear, in some way, to be useful. But to make these sorts of judgement, it is important for learners to be able to be explicit about their thoughts to enable self-monitoring of what and how they think.

Work in Australia has been documented (Baird and Mitchell, 1986) where youngsters are deliberately taught different strategies to focus their thinking and learning. PEEL (the Project to Enhance Effective Learning) is an on-going project in schools and in different areas of the curriculum (not just in science). The teachers involved produce a newsletter of progress and events (see *PEEL Seeds*, Appendix 2) and catalogue their ups and downs in everyday school life.

Closer to home, Shayer (1989) has described his work within Fuerstein's Instrumental Enrichment (IE) training. He has worked with pupils who are moderately educationally subnormal and, through a one-hour-a-day programme, demonstrated marked improvement in achievement. In the hour, the role of the teacher is to:

> assist the pupil to become aware of his or her own resources rather than to teach them algorithms . . . the idea is to put the control for the means of gathering and processing information in the hands of the pupils.

What all this work has in common is that teachers go out of their way to emphasize the skills and processes that are happening so that youngsters have labels by which to think and talk about their own learning. It is what Salomon and Globerson (1987) call 'mindfulness'. This mindfulness is a way of describing an awareness of problems, situations and ways of thinking about them. That is, deliberately working through different strategies and personal questions when faced with a learning task (What is it I know here? What is it that I want to get? What have I actually got? What else can I do?).

Analysis of problems

The analysis of problems can take place on at least two levels — relating to surface details or to the essence of the problems. Sometimes the surface details are all that is necessary — an analogy or metaphor can sometimes work easily with only the minimum of similarity between two sets of circumstances. Sometimes, though, the analogy can be at a deeper level. Kahney (1986) sets out two problems along the following lines:

> A small country is ruled by a dictator, from a strong fortress in the middle of the country, surrounded by farms and villages. Many roads radiate out from the fortress like the spokes of a wheel. To free the country, a great general raises an army on the border and decides that if all his army could attack the fortress it could be captured. However, he learns that the dictator has mined the roads in such a way that while small numbers of people can pass over the mines safely, a large force would blow the road, kill many men and render the route impassable. A full frontal attack is therefore out of the question.
> The general's solution is to divide his army into many small groups at the head of each road and, when the signal is given to attack, to charge the fortress safely and yet arrive at full strength, and overthrow the dictator.

A second problem is then presented like this:

> You are a doctor faced with a patient who has a malignant tumour in his stomach. The patient is delicate and surgery is not possible — yet the tumour must be removed to save the patient. Radiation treatment is possible if the intensity is sufficiently high to destroy the tumour. Unfortunately high-intensity radiation will also destroy much of the tissue through which it passes to reach the tumour. While low intensity can be used safely, it will not affect the tumour either. What solution can you, the doctor, adopt?

Kahney goes on to describe work on these kinds of problem by Gick and Hoylake (1980). The basic outcomes are that:

- not all problem-solvers, by any means, will see a direct relationship between these kinds of story;
- the vast majority of the people who were given these problems used the analogy to solve the doctor's problem only when they were given a hint that the two problems were related;
- however, once given the hint, most people could then solve the second problem successfully.

Kahney says:

> The striking thing about these [problems] is that they have nothing in common on the surface. In the one case the objects represented are things such as a hospital patient, a doctor, special rays and so on. In the other the objects are a dictator and a general, armies, mines, roads and villages. So there is difficulty in explaining how the mind is able to find correspondences between events which are, on the face of it, completely unrelated.

REINFORCING TRANSFER

It is sometimes assumed (see, for instance, Further Education Unit, 1982) that there are things called 'generic skills' that are transferable by definition, because they appear in a wide range of tasks. But, says the FEU:

> at the moment there is little general awareness of how this might be done, or how teaching might assist the process.

What is clear, however, is that the crux of this kind of teaching hinges on the choice of problem and the key focus the teacher wants to develop, so that pupils can be introduced to tasks which are arranged according to similarity of their elements, concepts, principles and strategies. A report by the Institute of Manpower Studies (1982), for instance, suggests that the learning of skill transfer is enhanced by:

1. Explicitly introducing students to the notion of transfer.
2. Making students aware of the skills that have the highest potential for transfer.
3. Ensuring that students are conscious of the skills they are acquiring; introducing students to tasks which are arranged according to similarity of elements, concepts, principles and learning strategies.

4. Teaching students by methods which facilitate comprehension.
5. Involving students in the learning process.
6. Making students aware of different types of learning and making them conscious of their own learning style.

Transferability, they say, means to:

bring about a flexibility of attitude and a willingness to learn, sufficient to cope with the future changes in technology and career.

Pupils need to:

1. develop a particular capacity in a particular context;
2. identify other contexts in which the capacity could be useful;
3. be given practice at applying relevant aspects of previous learning to a new situation;
4. identify other aspects at which they are likely to be successful on the evidence of this learning.

Translating some of these ideas into classroom practice means that, first, it is important to set out problems for the class so that they are clearly similar to ones tackled before. It helps, too, to tell everyone which other problems they are like, how and why. Explicitly introducing the problem this way enables and facilitates transfer of learning. This is not giving 'the answer' or stifling initiative—it may well be that the problem-solvers decide to ignore the parallels drawn and proceed anyway in their own directions. But it does give a starting point and will help to promote some key ideas.

At the end of the session it is important to list and describe the sorts of skill that have been used in solving the problem. This tends to reinforce success, even if the solution has not worked as well as desired. But just as important, this 'debriefing' sets up the opportunity for transfer of skills and understanding for the next problem-solving session. That is, it helps problem-solvers to carry over ideas if they are explicitly introduced to the notion of transfer, and that, particularly in problem-solving, it is the transfer of ideas that is important. By talking about particular skills it is possible to make students aware of the skills that have the highest potential for transfer. Beginning and ending sessions with a discussion of skills can ensure that pupils are conscious of the skills they are acquiring.

The essence of teaching for transfer, then, is to pick out some key focus before the session. This is because the learning can be pushed along very much faster if both teacher and problem-solver are aware of the main focus of the problem-solving session, and what is actually going on. For example, in general people learn through problem-solving better if they:

- recognize that the problem they are faced with is similar to one they have done before. This means they can decide what type of problem it is and what is needed as a solution, and can get started more easily;
- realize that they need to use some of the skills they have used before. Then they can carry over some of their skills and understanding more quickly;
- see where they can obtain more information and who and what is available to help them;
- appreciate what the constraints are: the rules, the time allowed, the tools, the materials and so on;
- are encouraged to be flexible so that they develop attitudes where they are willing to listen to the others, change their ideas and persist with a group task;
- understand how the success of the problem is going to be judged.

GENERATING IDEAS

As I pointed out earlier, the weakest link in all the problem-solving chains or cycles is the point where the generating of ideas is meant to happen. This is where previous solutions are recalled, similar solutions drawn out, and models, analogies and metaphors proposed. While not everyone is seen to be imaginative, it is possible to set a range of ways in which people can develop ideas, by transferring from one context to another. For example:

- Transfer by metaphor and analogy. Hofstader (1985), for instance, discusses ways in which ideas can given rise to others by *deliberately* posing semi-serious questions such as:
    What is to a triangle as a triangle is to a square?
    What is to a honeycomb as a knight's move is to a city grid?
    What is to Greece as the Falkland Islands are to Britain?
    What is to visual art as the fugue is to music?
    What is to a waterbed as ice is to water?
    What is to the United States as the Eiffel Tower is to France?
    What is to German as Shakespeare's plays are to English?

- Transfer by slippage. This is a similar process whereby we slip from one idea to another almost accidentally. Sometimes the variation takes place through a mistake in hearing ('Oh, I thought you said . . .') or by a speaker's mixing up words or mispronouncing them so that they trigger another idea in a listener. No doubt these are sometimes funny and can embarrass the listener or speaker, but some new idea is aired through the process. Drawings can be misrepresented and words in print can be misread ('For a moment I thought it looked like . . .'), and a slippage has occurred. One normally needs to be on the lookout for these and to see the potential in them when they happen.
- Young children's questions can be an excellent source of thought-provoking ideas. Fisher (1987) lists some as:

> Where do days go when they are over?
> If I have two eyes why don't I see two of you?
> How can we be sure everything isn't a dream?
> Can flowers be happy or sad?

- For some, there is no substitute for day-dreaming or doodling. Sketching ideas on paper can be an excellent way of setting ideas going. There is a huge literature on the study of 'imagery' and its role in thinking, generating ideas, understanding, forging concepts and so on. Arieti (1976) is just one author who explores the role of imagery in creativity; Miller (1986) has documented imagery in scientific thought.
- Developing variations on a theme. Trying to produce 'variations on a theme' is a time-honoured process. Most 'new' ideas are like this — their origins can be traced back to a previous set of ideas with just one or two changes. Many jokes and humorous stories happen in a similar way: one idea 'slips' into another and, sometimes, the variation goes so far that the original idea seems lost. Hofstader (1985) calls this 'playfully [to] explore serendipitious connection'. To do this deliberately is to vary conditions, varying one condition at a time to see what happens. When this process is exhausted, several conditions are varied together. As Hofstader says:

Are not variations on a theme somehow trivial, compared to the invention of the theme itself? This leads one back to the seductive notion that Einstein and other geniuses are 'cut from a different cloth' from ordinary mortals, or at least that certain cognitive acts done by them involve principles that transcend the everyday ones. This is something I do not believe at all. If you look at the history of science, for instance, you will see that every idea is built upon a thousand related ideas.

There is no doubt that this whole book could (or should) be devoted to the generation of ideas, since in many ways this lies at the very heart of problem-solving. I would like, though, to emphasize the following points:

- we can facilitate creativity in science, technology and problem-solving by encouraging it at the very start;
- we can encourage the development of ideas by structuring learning experiences to encompass progressively more complex or varied problems;
- we can encourage transfer of ideas by pointing out skills, processes and relationships, and rehearsing these through structured problems;
- we can enhance transfer of skills by being explicit about what they are and attempting the direct teaching of skills.

THE OWNERSHIP OF LEARNING

I now want to focus on the ownership of learning, since I believe that ownership, too, is a central feature of effective learning and transfer. The essence of ownership is that the problems are real and relevant for the problem-solvers; they are ones which they want to solve and for which they can take responsibility.

At the heart of the matter is, of course, a dilemma — how to engage pupils in (GIVEN, or GOAL) tasks which the teacher wants to take place in order that transfer can occur in certain directions, while at the same time allowing and encouraging pupils to generate and take ownership of their own (OWN) problems.

An example

A good example of a problem beginning as a GOAL problem and becoming an OWN one arose as follows. During an A-level physics class a student wanted to investigate the physics of smoke rings. Part of the A-level Nuffield Physics course is based on students' own investigations and so this seemed a useful topic. The student in question was sometimes hard to motivate and his interest in smoke rings seemed to stem more from his own attempts as a cigarette smoker than his fascination with physics. He designed a 'smoke ring generator' by covering the mouth of a glass beaker with plastic food-wrap, or cling-film. He burned a small, circular hole in the centre of the film. He then filled the beaker with smoke so that when he tapped the cling-film, the membrane of plastic moved up and down to send a string of perfectly symmetrical smoke rings up through the hole. Most students would have been content with exploring this little device but, during his experiments, he noticed something else. For each set of smoke rings propelled upwards into the air, he noticed a complementary set of 'clear air' rings which were sent down through the smoke remaining in the beaker. This was unexpected, a chance observation, and it immediately caught his imagination — he was the first, he declared, to discover 'negative', 'anti-smoke rings'.

At this point his investigations took a new turn. Instead of a beaker he used a long, clear Perspex tube as a 'clear ring' generator so that he could follow the air rings down the tube through the smoke. The tube gave him a good controlled environment for these rings: he counted the rings for a given 'tap' of the film, timed them, measured them, photographed them, and looked at a range of variables in what had become *his* discovery, *his* experiment and, of course, *his* results. As the problem increasingly became an OWN problem, his interest in solving it increased with the development of the solution.

Similar examples can be drawn from other contexts. White (1990), for instance, describes the enthusiasm of primary school pupils as they investigated which of the teachers' coffee mugs is the 'best', an investigation that sprang obliquely from their discussions about heat.

That said, there can be no magic formula for inveigling learners into problem-solving, except for giving them many opportunities to do so with the freedom, at times, to explore further.

A question at this stage of the chapter might be: To what extent are there discernible and differing models of ownership of learning within science classrooms? Presumably some pupils will arrive at the classroom with a range of their own independent ideas and questions which they are keen to work on themselves. Moreover, they will be resentful of attempts by the teacher to impose any other problem on them. Others will be happy to accept a problem wholesale from teacher and would feel adrift without hints, clues and, sometimes, direct help. Between these extremes there is probably a spectrum of approaches to problem-solving.

Essentially, this spectrum can be seen to extend across a range from 'strong' ownership cases to 'weak' ones, where 'strong' models of ownership might mean that *each individual in the class is responsible 100% for his/her own learning progress, and each individual in a problem-solving group is responsible 100% for the group's progress*, and 'weak' means *some personal gain in self-direction*. That is, it is a range against which it is possible to classify individuals' commitment to, and part ownership of, group tasks. How far can institutionalized ownership of learning take place in an ordinary classroom? Arguably,

> ownership of learning = power to negotiate
> + responsibility for knowledge-seeking
> + opportunity for development in varying contexts
> + actionable assessment
> + the right of veto

That is, to what extent can ownership of learning be exercised in the constraints of classrooms and schools?

As I try to set out some answer to these it is useful to take a brief look at the CREST Project. It is a national scheme to promote problem-solving, and is aimed at activities in science and technology (Watts and West, 1990). Its work might provide some insights into the ownership of learning.

CREST

The acronym CREST stands for CREativity in Science and Technology, a scheme sponsored by the Department of Education and Science and industry, and supported jointly by the British Association for the Advancement of Science (BA) and the Standing Conference on Schools Science and Technology (SCSST). It is co-ordinated at a local level through Science and Technology Regional Organizations (SATROs) and by some local education authorities. The entire project is basically an award scheme for rewarding youngsters' efforts in school—the project's primary aim is to promote scientific and technological problem-solving in the 11 to 18 age range. In this sense, it builds on the Young Investigators' scheme, also sponsored by the

BA, and which is targeted at the junior school age range, i.e. 8–12. Both schemes aim to complement normal schoolwork and are non-competitive: youngsters gain recognition for their work through the scheme as a national project, and receive a Bronze, Silver or Gold award (see Figure 4.1).

CREST awards are criterion referenced, and are part of a scheme designed to stimulate and support problem-solving activity. The scheme encourages (in its early phases) then requires (in its later phases) students to identify and work on OWN problems. These problems, though, are identified through an 'active partnership' between the students or school and the industrial/business community.

How, you might ask, can students be encouraged to identify their own problems? Much depends on the freedom to choose, and the flexibility of schools (and adaptability of teachers) in allowing students to pursue an investigative pathway, within limits.

CREST places considerable emphasis on 'problem identification', 'negotiation' and links between the student or schools and a range of outside agencies. Students are encouraged to develop their own strategies and (within the safety of the laboratory or workshop) are allowed to experience the successes (and failures) associated with project management. Negotiation at regular intervals over the criteria provides powerful insights for the students. They are not told what to do but are helped to achieve what they want in pursuit of their project objectives. The quality of the students' experiences is monitored using a profile. This asks them to provide evidence which they consider demonstrates the CREST process criteria. A series of 'You Can' statements on a record card maintained by both students and teachers points the way towards iterative problem-solving and successful project completion.

The three stages of the CREST award (Bronze, Silver and Gold) are addressed by an accumulating set of criteria — a ladder of achievement in problem-solving process skills (see Figure 4.2).

Therefore, a major point of the project is that youngsters work on their OWN project. Individually or in groups, the project is one that they choose. Teachers may be influential at the point of choice — as may the CREST local organizer — but the emphasis is heavily weighted towards the youngster designing his or her own investigation. At the end, students are required to explain the development and outcomes of their projects to the outside agencies who have supported their work. The scheme works equally well for both teams

British Association for the Advancement of Science (BA)
The Standing Conference on Schools' Science and Technology (SCSST)

SILVER AWARD
Presented to

For Creativity, Perseverance,
and the Application of Knowledge
in Science and Technology

Sir Alan Veale, Chairman

Crest is an activity of  and SCSST

Figure 4.1 An example of a CREST certificate.

CREST GOLD AWARD
PROFILE OF PROBLEM-SOLVING SKILLS

You and your teacher will meet on at least five occasions to talk about your project. At these meetings your progress will be assessed using the statements below.Each **goal or criterion** must be met on at least one occasion during the project. Of course, this does not apply if a particular criterion is not relevant to your investigation.

Name

Project Title

Project Consultant(s)_____ Individual ☐ Team ☐ Tick one box

You can	Number of times assessed					
	1	2	3	4	5	Optional
Produce a workable idea/ideas in response to the problem identified.						
Find out information to help you with your investigation. Liaise with your consultant.						
Transfer science/technology ideas from familiar to new situations.						
Show originality in how you understand and interpret the problem set and in the ideas you have for solving it.						
Select/reject possible ways of doing the investigation and explain your reasons.						
Design a fair test and predict what results you expect.						
Attempt to control several interacting variables.						
Use your results to find out if they fit the idea being tested.						
Explain what your observations or results tell you in the light of what you are trying to find out.						
Attempt to cross check your results and explain the results that do not agree with the predictions you made.						
Alter and improve your investigation in the light of what you have found out.						
Work carefully and accurately.						
Record different ways of doing your investigation explaining the strengths and weaknesses of each approach.						
Record and explain why there may be more than one explanation for what you found out.						
Understand in what ways your experiment or prototype might not work in a different situation i.e. prototype uncertainty/accuracy limitation of experiments						
Explain how far you got in your CREST Award project, what problems you found and how you tried to overcome them.						

Signature of Student_____ Date _____

Signature of Leader_____ Date_____

FINAL EVALUATION

The two sets of criteria are the goals which each student is meant to achieve during a project. It is the role of the Evaluator to make sure the goals relevant to the project have actually been met.

The first set of criteria have been used by the group leader to complete the Profile of Problem-Solving Skills.The profile will be used when the Final Evaluation is made.

The Evaluator will decide whether **the second set of criteria** have been achieved at end of the project.

You should expect to

Negotiate successfully with a consultant to mutually agree a project specification

Explain clearly your part in planning and carrying out the project using your own words.

Show that advice from a range of sources has been taken into account in problem generation, perception and reformulation.

Draw valid conclusions through an iterative approach to problem-solving.

Apply a wide range of concepts and skills precisely, using appropriate controls, to solve a real-life problem which meets a human need.

Explain how problems were overcome and alternative solutions reached.

Produce a clear and concise record of the project using technical language and style.

Demonstrate the fitness for purpose of the product of your work.

Suggest where appropriate, potential industrial/social/commercial applications of the project work.

Signature of Evaluator

Date

Figure 4.2 Criteria of the CREST Gold Award.

and individual students. This is particularly so at the level of Silver and Gold awards, where the scheme is looking for quite original (creative) work.

One of CREST's secondary aims is to promote closer working relationships between schools and engineering, industry and commerce in the outside world. Some projects have involved the electronics industry where, for example, youngsters have designed a 'seven-day pet-cat feeding system' so that the cat's owners can leave the pet well fed while they are on holiday; or a system for allowing only the owner's cat through the cat flap.

Two more examples

The work of CREST can be explored a little more by considering how it has been managed in two schools. The first is an example of how problem-solving was woven across the curriculum and timetabled over a period of time. The second case study describes how a school suspended the timetable to hold a problem-solving day.

Paper-making at St Peter's

This example is one of theme-based problem-solving activities. In a way, the theme was of the GIVEN type in that it arose from an art teacher's personal interest in paper-making. She wanted to bring paper-making into third-form art work, and this implied a degree of cross-curricular activity . This all-girl school was also keen to credit students' performance through the CREST Bronze award to reflect the technological process involved in the work.

Beyond this point, however, the girls developed ownership for their part of the project, the challenge being to make 'interesting' paper from available vegetable material. By selecting their own starting material (nettles, dock leaves, maize, lettuce, etc.!) they were able to stamp their individuality on the project, with the added stimulus of wanting to compare the 'fitness for purpose' of the various end-products. They were free to experiment with conditions such as:

- the extent to which the raw fibre was chopped;
- the time the fibre was steeped in sodium hydroxide solution;
- the effects of final pulp pH and pH correction.

Some of the student teams were involved in designing and making the equipment required for the process.

Having produced a number of samples of 'hand-made' paper, the students were keen to compare the physical properties of the products, such as strength and absorbency, against each other and against commercially produced paper. They went on to consider the aesthetic appeal of the materials for artistic purposes. They were also prompted to consider the marketability of their hand-made sheet paper as a result of the considerable interest generated through visitors to the school. It appeared they had produced a much sought-after commodity! Thus chemistry problem-solving emerged quite naturally as part of theme work, and involved progressively more and more curriculum areas within the school. The work used 'art time' — two lessons per week for a term — and was accredited through and supported by CREST.

Preparing amoxycillin

This second example is an industry-stimulated (and directed) practical activity concerning the laboratory synthesis of amoxycillin. It is also an example of a problem that was GIVEN and, at first sight, seems to require few problem-solving skills and little opportunity for innovative experimentation. A second look, though, reveals the tremendous range of learning opportunities that are possible.

The scene: a chemistry lab at a sixth-form centre south of London; a dozen white-coated sixth-formers working closely with an industrial chemist; a quiet intensity over racks of test-tubes as all concerned grapple with the problem — the preparation of amoxycillin. The students were working with the industrialist using techniques they had not previously encountered. For these youngsters, organic chemistry took on a different dimension; confidence in practical skills, together with communication skills in 'chemistry speak', were considerably enhanced. Some members of the class wanted to go further, to own more of the project and interact and experiment with a sophisticated chemical system. They were keen, for instance, to see the fruits of their labours — a week-long synthetic pathway leading to a collection of yellow crystals. Though satisfying in a number of respects, the results still begged the questions 'Is this what it's supposed to be?' and 'How did the original reagents end up as this product?'

The students chose to investigate their product through some of the analytical techniques available to them. They had the use of IR spectrometry and gas-liquid chromatography, and began to interact with the synthesis by attempting to look for evidence of structural changes as the reaction pathway proceeded. This extension to the original activity injected a different kind of stimulus into their work. The problem now was to produce evidence to support the string of reactions represented on paper, which, at the outset, had meant very little conceptually. Once started, they wanted to 'see' more and to model further. They became interested in the concept of molecular graphics and were introduced to the system used at the University of Surrey, where part of the CREST scheme is based. 'Suddenly organic chemistry became real,' said one.

The ability to model, rotate and add and subtract functional groups gave the freedom to experiment in chemistry, a freedom not previously imagined. The students were in control; they could hypothesize and produce evidence to support reaction pathways, and suggest mechanisms for stages in the process.

Inspired by benefits of this kind, the school has now been prompted to find resources to purchase equipment and software to support other areas of the chemistry curriculum, so that the ability to model and experiment with chemical structures is now available to all students of chemistry. In this sense, CREST was the catalyst to the development of chemistry extension work, by providing a stimulus encouraging students to question and investigate.

Key terms

So what are the key terms to come out of the CREST scheme? For me, they are:

- OWN problem-solving;
- technologically relevant problems;
- the involvement of commerce and industry, and 'adults other than teachers' (AOTs) within the classroom;
- problem identification and negotiation;
- the potential for self- and peer assessment.

There is no doubt for me that the *potential* for ownership of the problems is on the 'strong' side of my divide, in that each individual in the class is responsible for his/her own learning. The contract in terms of Bronze, Silver or Gold is with the individual and the teacher and/or AOT uses the CREST problem criteria as vehicles for discussion with the problem-solver of progress made. Where youngsters are in groups then any outcomes that are developed are the product of the group's work and so each individual is also responsible for the group's progress. Similarly, through this sort of scheme, ownership of learning *does* involve the power to negotiate, responsibility for knowledge-seeking, the opportunity for tackling varying contexts, an opportunity to take part in the process of assessment.

ACTIVE LEARNING

In Bentley and Watts (1989) we attempted to identify the characteristics of learners who had 'made learning their own'. We decided they are learners who:

- initiate their own activities and take responsibility for their own learning;
- make decisions and solve problems;
- transfer skills and learning from one context to other different contexts;
- organize themselves and organize others;
- display their understanding and competence in a number of different ways;
- engage in self- and peer evaluation;
- feel good about themselves as learners.

By the last of these was meant that the task in hand, or the scheme of work, is something *they* want to do. It often comes from within them, for their need to know or to find a solution. It may be that the impetus or suggestion for it comes from the teacher or from outside the classroom, like the smoke ring example earlier. Nevertheless, the learner wants to shape it so that it becomes his or her task, and consequently the learner becomes accountable for its outcomes. This way the learner feels in control and fully involved in his/her own learning.

Active learners can recognize the demands of particular tasks, take responsible decisions and seek ways to solve problems within them. That is, they are able to judge the task for what it is worth, and tackle it appropriately, even when it derives from outside, from a scheme of work, from the teacher or from some other source. Making decisions is important; it is only when learners make decisions towards the solution of a problem that they begin to own the problem for themselves.

This depiction of active learners includes the idea that they develop feelings of ownership over information, data, interpretations and understandings, which means that they can begin to judge the worth of facts and opinions. Ownership is important because it indicates that the learning taking place is, as Strike and Posner (1985) suggest, intelligible, credible, fruitful and relevant to the youngsters concerned.

Active learning means being able to work independently *and* work within a group. It is an important attribute of active learners that they know when a task is one to be tackled alone or one that requires collaboration with others. Working individually, or working closely with others in a small group, does involve particular skills and abilities. Such skills enable individuals to become co-operative members of the community. Active learners are also aware of the time require-ments of different tasks and are capable of pacing themselves to meet deadlines. They use a range of study skills, and select the most appro-priate resources and information and the means of gaining access to them. This means that youngsters select the most appropriate means of reporting their progress, what they know and understand. In discus-sions they are able to communicate and explain their ideas and understandings so that others can appreciate them. In doing so they tailor their report to match their audience, showing an awareness of what style is appropriate.

Active learners are effective learners. That is, they are confident enough to develop their own criteria, evaluate their own progress regularly and recognize their own competence and weaknesses. They are prepared to share these criteria and evaluations of their progress with their peers and teachers. They are willing to discuss them, defend them and where necessary review them in the light of others' opinions. They are also prepared to assist in the evaluation of others' progress and share those evaluations with the individuals concerned in a non-threatening and supportive way.

Finally, active learners believe in themselves and grow in enthusiasm for what they are doing. They understand that learning is an emotional business, involving excitement, disappointment, sudden 'eureka' moments and periods of perseverance. Because they are engaged in establishing their own directions and progress, they are more likely to divine success in what they do. Success breeds confidence and, in turn, confidence breeds positive feelings and motivation.

In the same way, it is also important to identify some of the ingredients necessary for active learning. Among them are:

- a non-threatening learning environment;
- pupil involvement in the organization of the learning process;
- opportunities for learners to take decisions about the content of their own learning;
- direct skill teaching;
- continuous assessment and evaluation;
- relevance and vocationalism.

Active learners are involved in speculation, experimentation and reformulation of their ideas and existing concepts. Such activities require emotional investments. The process of sharing and reforming ideas — admitting that one has not understood something thoroughly, for example — is often quite difficult. It can sometimes be accompanied by ridicule from peers and/or the teacher. Youngsters may then be reluctant to engage with the whole process. Consequently the environment in which youngsters propose and test out ideas needs to be supportive, while still giving honest evaluation of their efforts. They need to grow and change through this evaluation, yet they also need to be sure that such evaluation will concentrate upon their 'professional' contribution, not demean them as individuals.

Early involvement in the way the lesson, scheme or tasks are to be organized maximizes the possibilities of active learning. It allows learners to begin to stamp their own direction on what is taking place, orientate the activities to their own needs and influence events so that they feel they have some purpose for them. In this, early pupil involvement allows teachers and pupils to establish some common goals about how learning is to take place.

Growth towards independent autonomous learning means giving pupils opportunities to choose what they learn and how they display their learning to others. They need also to be able to evaluate their own learning, and decide about further directions.

Many of the attributes of active learning need to be taught directly, in effect to be tutored. For example, while it is important to provide opportunities for participative group work, some of the skills of co-operation and negotiation involved in working in a group need to be taught directly. This is also the case for some study skills, as well as particular scientific skills.

For learners to develop a realistic sense of their own worth, and the value of their ideas, they must be involved in evaluation of those ideas as they progress. Such involvement enables them to diagnose their strengths and weaknesses, and take their own steps to build on them, or rectify them.

In this view, active learning needs to be relevant learning. It may well be possible to use alternative approaches in the classroom: for example, to have youngsters memorize an obscure set of nonsense syllables in an 'active' way, play 'Trivial Pursuit' in order to accumulate facts on 'science and nature', or enact party-game charades of famous personalities in chemistry. However, alternative methods alone are not sufficient to engender active learning. Such methods only really become active when they have a purpose; when they achieve relevance by being set within the context of everyday life and the world of work and leisure. The intention here is not to endorse narrow vocationalism, an ethos of producing 'cannon fodder for industry', but to see learning in the broader sense of exploring the ways of the world — and within that, to take the world of work as an important site of study and experience.

Chapter 5

Classroom Management and Changing the Curriculum for Problem-Solving

INTRODUCTION

In this chapter I want to draw together some of the implications of organizing and managing problem-solving within school activities. The discussion is based on themes from earlier chapters:

- Problem-solving promotes active learning, on behalf of both teacher and pupil.
- Teachers who come new to problem-solving emerge as very active learners themselves. The change of role required to cope with open-ended problem-solving can mean a rapid reappraisal of self and function.
- Youngsters enjoy problem-solving and there is every evidence that active learning does take place. As Wallwork (1989) says:

  The pupils seemed to respond to the relevance of the problem and worked tirelessly . . . through normal breaks . . . plans were modified and in some cases changed radically in an attempt to produce a demonstrable solution before the end of the day.

  And, in almost a throwaway line, he adds:

  At the end of the day the children shared their solutions, demonstrating their devices with boiling water and blindfolds. Everyone produced a device and was given praise from peers and adults.

- The real reward for most of the youngsters is being able to design their own experiments and work in their own way — to own what they are doing. That helps to ensure that the problems are relevant and produce high levels of motivation.

- Ownership is paramount, not only for obvious motivational reasons but also because ownership of problems means personal designation of parts of the curriculum.

METHODS OF TEACHING AND LEARNING

How the teacher of science and technology chooses to construct 'learning experiences' for pupils is a matter of professional choice. In their interim report (1987), and reinforced by the National Curriculum Council (1989a), the Science Working Party want teachers on each occasion to ask will the experience:

- stimulate curiosity?
- give opportunity for developing attitudes relating to scientific and technological activity, including curiosity and co-operative learning?
- give opportunity for developing basic science concepts?
- relate to the interests of children at a particular age and to their everyday experiences?
- appeal to both boys and girls and to those of all cultural backgrounds?
- help children understand the world around them through their own mental and physical interaction with it?
- give opportunities to work co-operatively and to communicate scientific ideas to others?

These can be difficult criteria to satisfy at the best of times, given that many teaching groups will have a number of approaches to learning, a variety of aptitudes and a range of attitudes to the matters in hand. That is, any class has within it some thirty or so individuals, all of whom come to lessons with different needs, predilections, prior models, preferred modes of learning and so on. These are not constant and can change even as the session progresses. The best solution for one learner might be anathema to another. We know there has been no teaching strategy invented yet that has guaranteed universal appeal, no matter what the topic area. Moreover, every teacher, too, comes with certain strengths and predispositions — there has been no 'teacher proof' method invented either.

As has been suggested elsewhere (Bentley and Watts, 1989), the upshot of all this is that teachers must continue to develop a wide range of teaching strategies to cater for the diversity of personal experience and differentiation of individual attainment found in any class. Since one single strategy will not work for all occasions, teachers must be able to draw on many – to move constantly between, modify, add to and refine a comprehensive 'tool box' of methods. Practical explorations, role-play, small-group discussions, problem-solving, debates, Young Engineers' Clubs, mime, CREST projects, industrially produced materials, video-making, egg-races, fieldwork, creative writing, design-and-make activities, drama – these are some of the many possibilities that exist in science and technology, as in any other part of the curriculum.

In broad terms, and from what has been said in earlier chapters, the steps teachers might take, then:

> lie in our helping the learners themselves to gain insights into the processes of their own minds and learning processes. For teachers, the fruits of this insight would be the ways that they become conscious of, and recognise the effect and impact of, their children's own approaches to science study. The hoped for result would be that these learners are then more able to take responsibility for their own learning

and we might say that:

> self-understanding can expand the realm of choices and possibilities which we see available to us to cope in the life situation in which we find ourselves. (Shapiro, 1988)

That is, to interact effectively with students might be to help them articulate and recognize their own ideas, to share these with others and to listen to and appreciate other people's models for the same phenomena. Further, interaction may enable students to strengthen their thinking; it may perhaps demonstrate the difference between their views and the scientific one; it may indicate the strengths and weaknesses of both points of view; and may help explore ways in which the students can test the plausibility and fruitfulness of their own ideas.

ESTABLISHING PROBLEM-SOLVING

It is best to start in primary schools, some say, to infuse the curriculum with problem-solving. For example:

The ability to recognise, analyse and solve problems is now receiving recognition as an essential part of all children's intellectual development. The most appropriate point to start this education is in the primary phase.

(Williams and Jinks, 1985)

Williams and Jinks' 'Pentagonal Model' (Figure 5.1) is an example of how they see technology and design (and thus a problem-solving approach) as lying across the primary curriculum. In the model, the primary school curriculum is depicted as comprising five main areas: language and literacy; mathematics; science; social studies; aesthetic and physical education. Williams and Jinks see design and technology as the agent for unification:

Design technology in the primary school is an exciting and motivating activity. Through careful planning and sympathetic teaching, design and technology can forge links between the classroom and the real world that exist outside the boundaries of the school.

Design and technology may (or may not) be a 'unifying concept' for all schools; there are others. However, to arrive at the point where all (or most) teachers in a school share views on technological problem-solving is not particularly easy. So, let me begin at the beginning, where teachers come together. Their first step is to swap opinions and begin to establish a policy for what they want to do. This might involve the following stages:

- a group of teachers (from a single year-group or department, or from several) decide on what *they* mean by problem-solving;
- they discuss the reasons for introducing problem-solving in their curriculum areas. They consider their aims and objectives (they may wish initially to use those provided by others);
- they identify exactly what concepts, skills and attitudes they wish to establish. They may have recourse to some of the lists identified in Chapter 2;
- they work out all the organizational factors that will facilitate the policy;
- they sketch out the resource implications of doing problem-solving;
- they outline how they will evaluate the sessions afterwards.

As Williams and Jinks (1985) point out, this kind of process then gives rise to a series of questions on each of the resources involved, questions that are considered below.

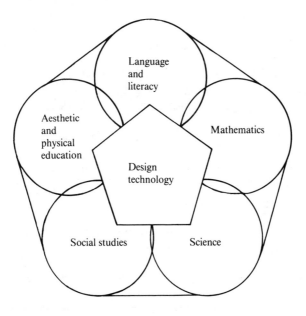

Figure 5.1 The Pentagonal Model illustrating the relationship between design/technology and the primary curriculum. Source: Williams and Jinks (1985).

Resources

Human resources

Will you involve people from outside the school (AOTs: adults other than teachers) — parents, governors, local (or national) industries? What will be their role? Will you give them guidance before they engage with pupils? Are there other problem-solving groups around? Are other schools tackling work in this way?

Materials

All practical work requires pre-planning. Some of the obvious aspects of problem-solving concern:

- trying to guess what kind of special apparatus or materials will be needed;
- getting hold of a large amount of consumable items like string, Sellotape, scissors, glue, cardboard and so on;
- predicting what text and visual material will be needed to stimulate ideas;
- designing 'clue cards', safety instructions, pre-reading, homework, etc.;
- planning the timing, technical support, room layout, disposal of waste; planning the teachers' change of role;
- selecting tools that are appropriate in size and kind: are they in good condition, and easily available? Are work surfaces suitable? Have safety procedures been established for access and use of the tools?

There are further questions. What materials will be needed? Wood, plastic, metal, wire, card, concrete, rubber, paper, electronics? And small items — propellers, motors, batteries, wheels, pulleys, cogs? Where and how will these be stored? What books, slides, videos, catalogues, etc. do you have around to support the tasks envisaged?

In some cases the problem of apparatus can be overcome by stipulating that the problem has to be solved using the equipment available or with apparatus provided by the youngsters themselves. One approach is to order more materials than seem necessary but hold them back in the wings so as not to overawe some of the groups or individuals.

Organization of time and physical space is important. As in project work, youngsters may want to store work from one day to the next, and to have access to it in between times. Allowing them to do so needs flexibility and co-operation within the department, the technical support staff and the school as a whole. Apparatus may need to be ordered directly by youngsters and this needs a robust and responsive system that can cope with vagaries and omissions. One suggestion is to try to ensure that problems are do-able in the time allotted, that the time allowed is generous or that there is a circus of problems. This raises the following points:

Time

Are there arrangements that might prevent children having uninterrupted periods of time? Can work be carried over or will tasks have to fit completely the allotted time? How will you help pupils plan their time?

Space

Where will half-completed models and half-used materials be kept? How will classrooms be organized? Will tools be stored easily and safely? There must be opportunity, too, for youngsters to be able to display their wares by demonstrating their outcomes. There is often sufficient variety in the solutions to make the end performance entertaining as well as rewarding. Photographs can be taken during the session and these can be posted as soon as they are printed. Posters, flip charts or overhead projector transparencies are obvious ways to report outcomes and can be well designed to illustrate the processes that were undertaken and the results achieved.

Organizing problems

Further questions: do you set the same problem for a whole class group so that they generate different solutions? Do you set one large problem to all and ask different groups to tackle different aspects so that you build up a composite picture at the end? Do you set different problems for different groups, or even a different problem for each individual and allow them to work separately?

The real reward for most of the youngsters is being able to design their OWN experiments and work in their own way — to own what they are doing. It is a way of helping to ensure that the problems are personally and corporately relevant and produce high levels of motivation.

Where in the curriculum?

The answer is: anywhere. There are encouraging signs that problem-solving is increasingly an acceptable way of working in maths, home economics, geography, history and other less usual areas of the curriculum. Although I focus on science and technology in this book, this does not mean that problem-solving starts and ends there.

I have already noted that the sort of technologically orientated, industrially related problem-solving described in Chapter 4 is a considerable departure from traditional school problem-solving. It is part of a movement that includes the notions of 'Industrial Uncles and Aunts'; Young Engineers' Clubs; Enterprise Initiatives; Summer Schools, and so on. It is seen as an important way of developing young scientists' and technologists' skills, as well as providing (sometimes) fierce motivation, industrial contacts, personal and classroom relevance and other benefits besides.

A closer look at some of the practice of problem-solving in schools provides an interesting picture. My own experiences suggest that, of the problems chosen to be solved in school science, it is problems in physics and technology that predominate. Biological problems do feature, but chemical problems are few and far between. As I have noted elsewhere (Watts and West, 1990), chemists have come somewhat late to the scene and have yet to make a serious impact on problem-solving in schools. Perhaps this is because problem-solving has come into science through physics or craft design and technology (both often avowedly unchemical!). There could be other reasons, of course: perhaps many more 'real-life' problems are susceptible to mechanical, physical or biological solutions than they are to chemical ones. Or perhaps chemical techniques require a higher entry level than other routes. Interesting questions, then, might be: does chemistry simply have fewer problems embedded in it than other areas of science? Are the 'interesting' problems in chemistry inaccessible to school pupils? Are chemical problems just too difficult, or simply more numerical? Or, is it that there *are* good and interesting problems in chemistry but teachers and learners normally shy away from them and so need to be drawn into them?

Munson (1988) has coined the phrase 'curriculum-dedicated problems' for problems that have arisen from work currently in progress within the curriculum. Hence a 'chemical problem' is any problem that uses knowledge in chemistry towards a solution. The amount of chemistry can vary: the problem might have several solutions that are entirely chemically based or, alternatively, there might be only a modicum of chemistry involved. For instance, some problems within biotechnology may have a component that involves the student in determining pH, and the effects that variation in pH will have on the final outcomes. Alternatively the problem may be set within a 'chemical context'. This is most easily seen when industry becomes involved with the school in the problem-solving process.

So, to represent the chemists in this process of problem-solving, the list below is taken from the CREST data files of problems already being tackled at various points in chemistry lessons:

1. Saponification: the problems of making soap.
2. Testing the difference between biological and non-biological washing powder.
3. What are the causes of fading in blue jeans?
4. Paper making—what are the properties of laboratory-prepared paper?
5. What are pheromones? Looking at synthesizing pheromones at the school laboratory level.
6. The extraction and identification of antibiotics from lichen.
7. Superconductivity—the production of the ceramic.
8. Antibiotic production using a biofermenter.
9. Extraction of metals from minerals—the applications of microbial metal leaching.
10. The corrosion-inhibiting effects of quaternary ammonium compounds.
11. A study of metalloenzymes.
12. An assessment of water purity.
13. The vanadium and nickel concentrations in heavy fuel oils.
14. The conditions of fermentation—farm effluents and their use for the production of methane.

Where to problem-solve?

Back to the nitty gritty. Problem-solving as an educational activity is not confined to school buildings, but it is in schools that it generally takes place. Any space within the school may be appropriate: laboratory, workshop, assembly hall, gym, classroom. The room will depend on the kind of problem-solving and the resources needed. Sometimes a lot of room is needed. For instance, 'to make a parachute that falls as slowly as possible' needs somewhere high but safe from where to drop the parachute. The balcony in the assembly hall might be suitable, or the wall bars in the gym. To 'make a paper aeroplane that flies as far as possible in a straight line' needs a long space; a school corridor might be best.

But clearly, problem-solving can take place outside school. The making can be done at home or at a clubhouse; the testing can be done at a local factory or works.

Some problems need a lot of resources, tools and equipment. For example:

> Design and construct an electrically driven vehicle to cover a course 15 metres long. During its journey, the vehicle must be steered remotely through electrical control wires. At three points on its journey the vehicle is required to burst balloons suspended from the ceiling at a centre height of 300 mm above floor level.

This kind of egg-race problem will need wheels, gears, motors, electrical components and a power supply, and somewhere for it to be constructed. Ideally there would be space to store the work while it is in progress. The course, too, needs to be set out somewhere with space (15 metres is quite long).

What age range?

Problems can be introduced at a very early age. Some problems are suitable for children in infant schools; for instance:

> Convey a 'passenger' (made of pipe-cleaners or drinking straws) by water across a 'river' 3 metres wide.

Others are more appropriate for older students in the fifth form:

> Design and construct an air-driven car, to be powered by the air from a separate wind generator.

I noted earlier that some problems, such as some of the separation problems, can be used across the age range: there is some aspect of the problem that is suitable for different ages and abilities. For instance the traditional egg-race of transporting an egg using 'only the energy of a rubber band' can be done by anyone. The world record, by the way, is 368.29 metres!

In secondary schools, problem-solving has drawn teachers from many different subject areas: science and CDT, as well as maths, English, PE and music. Teachers there have found the experiences highly enjoyable, working with youngsters in an atmosphere very different from that of usual lessons. Some schools, of course, have entered staff teams into competitions so that they do not just organize and supervise but put their own ideas and teamwork to the test.

ORGANIZING PROBLEM-SOLVING IN SCHOOLS

This section looks at some of the many different ways in which problem-solving can be organized in schools, and considers some ways in which teachers have built problem-solving into the curriculum. The main ways are:

- problem-solving as an annual event
- problem-solving throughout the year
- problem-solving in the curriculum.

Problem-solving as an annual event

For some schools, problem-solving has been developed as part of a local or national competition. Most local egg-race events (like the Esso Problem Solving Challenge) are annual events, when teams compete to produce solutions to the kinds of problem that have already been suggested. Rather than enter teams without any previous experience, teachers usually organized various school activities beforehand, so that the youngsters have some idea of what is involved before the day itself. These events might be a competition organized by others — or they might be part of a school's 'activity week' towards the end of a summer term. Joining someone else's competition is always easier than running one's own, but there are lots of benefits in running activities in one's own school.

Organizing activity days

Increasingly, schools are giving over part of the timetable in the summer term to 'activity time'. This is usually a couple of days or a week when normal lessons are suspended and youngsters are allowed to opt for certain disparate activities taking up the whole day. Some activities continue for a whole week, others are for a day at a time; youngsters move from one to another. Problem-solving can fit either bill. It is possible to have a small set of problems that last for a protracted period of time, a large number that occupy a day each, some that are only an hour long, or some combination of these.

Large problems

Large problems begin to assume the proportions of 'projects' and take quite some planning. Designing and making a remote-controlled vehicle that must follow a prescribed path and undertake certain actions *en route* would certainly take a few days' hard work. More ambitious ideas often require the expertise of individuals outside the school: local or national industry, commerce, experts, industrial facilities, materials and so on. Usually, too, they involve more than one school department, involve quite a lot of materials (and therefore expense) and take up a lot of space. If that sounds off-putting, it shouldn't. Once youngsters get started on a substantial problem it can become all-consuming and the rewards are immense. They seldom have the time, or freedom, within schools to devote all their creative energies to one task over several days and the results are very worthwhile. So, for large problems:

- be prepared;
- sort out some financial support and materials in advance and some way of gaining access to small sums of money as it is needed;
- sections of the school will need to be reserved for the problem-solvers for a period of time;
- the pupils will need to have access to different parts of the school at different times of the day, and so the teacher will need the support of colleagues and the whole school in the tasks;
- the venue will need to be prepared for the final challenge between the teams.

One-day problems

There are a large number of problems that are suitable for solving within one day. Some examples are given in Appendix 1 and in the books cited in the Bibliography. The day might stand on its own in the school year as a one-off event, or it may be one of several activity days at the end of the year.

ORGANIZATION INTO PRACTICE – SOME EXAMPLES

Activity days

There are a number of ways in which schools have organized 'activity' days. Two examples follow.

School A

The head of CDT at School A decided that the department would organize problem-solving for one day of the year. He began with:

- permission from the headteacher and the rest of the school that all of this could happen;
- a small sum of money from the department's allocation;
- the time of other members of staff who agreed to help supervise;
- the co-operation of the technical support staff and the school keeper;
- deciding it would be for sixty second-year pupils who were not involved with another school activity that day.

The date was set and the department decided on two separate egg-races on the same day so that youngsters had some choice. Half the pupils (six groups of five) would do one; half the other.

The department decided which workshops and rooms would be used and which staff were to be based where, and organized all the appropriate equipment and materials. The day began with all the second-year pupils in the assembly hall, where they were asked to choose which problem to tackle and who their teams were to be. There then followed some arm-twisting and leg-pulling to ensure that the teams were roughly equal.

Once in their base rooms, work began and became so all-consuming that break was missed and there was a queue to get started early after lunch. The department had initially been concerned about allowing movement between the rooms – it would create problems should some of the pupils decide they had free run of the school buildings and become too boisterous. The workshop area of the school was relatively self-contained, and one member of staff acted as a sort of 'sweeper' to ensure that all pupils out of class were on proper errands. As it happened they need not have worried and the pupils stayed 'on-task' all day. The finale took place back in the hall as both competitions were played out and the winners were applauded and rewarded.

School B

The main organizer at School B was was the head of science. She decided to have a wide range of problems available, to allow pupils a choice of task. The department worked with the full set of ninety third-year pupils, and used some of the lessons in the run-up to the day to sort out the groups and problems. Some lessons after the day were used to evaluate the results.

She started with:

- permission from the headteacher and the rest of the school that all of this could happen;
- a small sum of money made up from the school fund and the local science adviser;
- the assistance of members of staff from other departments (English, Home Economics and Maths) who wanted to co-operate and get involved;
- interest from some individuals from outside the school, including one of the school governors, who came along for the day.

The pupils chose from a menu of problems, decided on their groups and began their planning in the weeks before the problem-solving day. One double lesson about a fortnight before was devoted to planning so that there was time for the groups to develop ideas and find any unusual materials well in advance. Two groups took up 'support' roles: one acted as a mini-enterprise company and (with a Home Economics teacher) organized the catering for the day; the other produced a newspaper of the day's events with two members of the English department. The first made a substantial profit, the second managed to desk-top edit their prose and then fax their text to the local newspaper office.

On the day, the problem-solvers knew pretty much what they had to do and worked in their own base rooms. The two support teams wore special badges and were allowed a roving brief so that they could achieve their tasks. Towards the end of the day the challenge was played out in separate classrooms. Each group was then allowed to visit the problems (and solutions) in other rooms to see what had been happening elsewhere. The lessons in the following week were used to evaluate fully the solutions that had been reached – and the problem-solving approach itself.

The drip-feed approach

Having problem-solving as a one-off or annual event is not enough for some: there is a determined mood to try to introduce the skills of problem-solving throughout the curriculum. Problem-solving does not have to be confined to science and technology although, as already noted, the main focus tends to be in those two areas.

There are several models of how schools have integrated problem-solving further into the curriculum. 'Drip-feed' is a term (Surrey SATRO, 1989) that might describe problem-solving that takes place at several points in the school year, mostly when it can be fitted in. That is not always the case, and some schools manage to work egg-races into their curriculum quite carefully. An example follows.

School C

School C has a problem-solving module as one of the first activities when youngsters arrive at the school in the first year. The module is called 'Being a Scientist' and is a conscious effort to introduce the skills of problem-solving early in their school career. It lasts for about five weeks and consists of a 'circus' of problems that all the class attempt.

School C's way of organizing work has several distinctive features:

- 'learning stations'
- the 'bit box'
- short, but linked, problems.

The staff work hard at selecting the problems to be used because they want to introduce these new first-year pupils to several particular practical skills, such as weighing and measuring in the laboratory, in a way that is subsumed within the problem. Therefore, the problems tend to revolve around some basic skills and some standard pieces of equipment. Around the laboratory are

'Learning Stations' so that when a group need the top-pan balance, for instance, they are directed to the appropriate station where there are explicit step-by-step instructions on how it is to be used.

There are five problems in the module and twenty pupils in the whole group. In each lesson, two pairs tackle each problem, with a play off towards the end of the lesson. As the weeks go by, the problems are modified slightly by changing the constraints (to go further, faster, longer, etc.) so that the element of challenge is retained and the next group have to improve on what the last lot achieved.

Most of the materials come from household items—it is 'yoghurt pot technology'. The youngsters are asked to bring in items from home and these are gathered in the 'bit box' in the lab—an old tea-chest in the corner.

School D

Some schools use lessons at the end of a module or particular section of work which they turn over to problem-solving. The example here comes from School D.

All of the science in the lower school at School D is 'modularized': the pupils do modules lasting roughly half a term each such as 'Flight', 'Water', 'Acids and Bases', 'Time' and so on, in years one to three. Each module ends with a piece of assessment, usually the obligatory test, and a problem-solving session. Here the pupils have to put into practice things they have learned in the module. Incidentally, the staff have become increasingly aware that it is possible to assess practical skills as the problem-solving takes place.

In the 'Flight' module, for example, the problem might be to build a model aircraft weighing not more than 100 grams which will remain airborne for as long as possible. In the 'Time' module the youngsters are asked to design and build a single device that will accurately measure both 30 seconds and a two-minute interval. The other problems range from building structures, designing a diver that can remain stationary at a point within some water (not on the surface), making windmills that would . . . and so on. Each of the problems have the same sort of constraints: 'within the set time', 'with the materials available', '1 metre off the ground' or whatever other rules apply. The problems are stated in the classroom materials, and so the pupils can look ahead to see what the problem will be in forthcoming modules. They can, if they want, begin planning well in advance. It is fair to say that the anticipation creates tremendous enthusiasm.

As in other schools, there is a bit box, and pupils make regular collections of normal household packaging items for their materials.

Curriculum-dedicated problem-solving

As noted earlier, this kind of problem-solving is tailored to the particular aspects of the curriculum being tackled at the time. It is similar to the drip-feed methods mentioned, but is different in two main respects:

- The sessions are not strictly timetabled into a module or a particular time of year; they happen more frequently and are not necessarily part of a set piece of work. That is, they occur as and when the work allows it.
- The sessions are not always programmed in advance and the selection of the problems is more a 'way of thinking' about practical work than a set of conscious decisions.

For example:

School E

Several members of School E Science Department are veteran egg-racers: two of them actually took part in one of the BBC's original programmes as part of a team. They now habitually set practical problems as 'egg-race' problems wherever they possibly can in the curriculum. So, for instance, a question in a fourth-year physics textbook might be worded 'Draw a pulley system with a velocity ratio 3. What load can be raised by an effort of 500 N if the efficiency is 75%?' This would normally be a calculative problem. There might be some practical work where pupils look at pulley systems and newtonmeters and (usually) fill in a chart of results. Instead, in School E, the question is turned into a problem: 'Using the materials available, design and build a system to get a 100 gram mass to raise 1 kilogram up through 30 centimetres.' The problem is turned into an egg-race challenge by amending the words to 'raising 1 kilogram by using the smallest mass you can'. The materials are usually the same pulleys, string, newtonmeters and assorted bits that might have been used anyway. However, the egg-race allows all sorts of other factors to come into consideration, questions to be asked, problems to be raised.

Similarly, a textbook question might be used that asks the pupils to 'Draw and label a diagram of a solar furnace'; 'Describe why a shiny teapot stays hotter than a dull, brown one'; or 'Explain why fire-fighting suits are made of shiny material'. There is nothing intrinsically wrong with questions like that, it is just that at School E they are often the prompt for some practical work and another excuse for problem-solving. The question might become 'Design and construct a solar water-heating system to increase the temperature of 2 litres of water in half an hour.' Obviously, the solution to that kind of question takes much more time than a 'draw-and-answer' response, but it usually takes the place of the practical work they would normally do—which is simply presented in a different way. Sometimes the planning and design is set for homework, some-times—if the problem is suitable—the whole task can be done at home.

Problem-solving does not take place *all* the time; merely as often as it can be managed. It is more a case of having a particular way of thinking about practical work that can be applied to almost anything in the science curriculum. In this sense the problems grow out of the curriculum and are not 'stuck in' in a way that can sometimes seem false.

School F

The opportunities to involve problems in the curriculum can extend beyond the usual science and CDT lessons. At School F, a sixth-form centre, teachers feel strongly that their TVEI (Technical and Vocational Educational Initiative) Extension work should be an integral part of the curriculum rather than a 'bolt-on' feature. They are trying to change all the syllabuses in time to take account of the implications of their TVEI Extension work, including their A-level syllabuses. The centre offers a core of foundation studies to all students; about 100 Foundation Studies courses are offered. Students are guided towards a balanced choice of courses by their tutor, encompassing the practical (computing, photography, sculpture), academic (psychology, history, a modern language) and community service. Problem-solving is included in the practical area and is a popular choice. It is also a regular feature of the Certificate of Pre-vocational Experience (CPVE) work at the Centre.

In the foundation work problem-solving began life with a 'Let's Build a Robot' course. First attempts to launch straight into a sophisticated working robot were not satisfactory because many of the students came with varied experience and expertise, and frustration rapidly developed when they could not achieve success quickly. The course leaders therefore had to devise several 'lead in' activities that would allow skills and expertise to be developed within a (very) mixed-ability group and yet maintain interest. They began with short problems and then graduated to tasks that required greater control of the device being made. For instance, an intermediate problem is to 'Design and construct a working model to lower a mass of 5 kilograms in a controlled manner from rest through a vertical distance of 1.5 metres to the floor in exactly 1.5 minutes.'

A 'whole problem' approach

There are a few schools at which people want to turn over most of their curriculum to a problem-solving approach. This happens more in some subject departments than in others, but sometimes the trend is throughout the school. It can be seen more easily in those subjects that have a practical basis, like science and home economics, but it has also penetrated to history and geography. In other schools one or two departments lead the way and 'do their own thing' regardless of what other parts of the school are doing, hoping that the others will follow suit.

School G

In School G the members of the CDT department are trying to work towards a 'whole problem-solving approach'. They have been involved in egg-race challenges over a number of years and many of the youngsters have acquired a degree of expertise. The curriculum has been set out as a series of design-and-make problems which the pupils are asked to tackle. The skills and knowledge that they need are taught as and when they are needed — sometimes on an individual basis, sometimes on the basis of small groups. In some cases the whole class stops work so that instruction can follow. In some instances, where one youngster has achieved a particular skill, he or she is asked to show someone else how to do it, so co-operative peer learning becomes the norm.

The problems used tend to be long-term ones and are chosen so that they allow a range of skills to be developed over time.

Other initiatives

The seven examples of schools, considered above, represent only some of the ways in which problem-solving can be incorporated into the curriculum. It is possible, even from my own experiences of watching problem-solving in action, to document many more. For instance, many schools use the Young Investigators and/or the CREST scheme as an after-hours science club; some build problem-solving whole-heartedly into the coursework for GCSE for both science and technology, and I have already mentioned the Young Engineers' Clubs, Summer School activities and so on.

Most recently the World Wide Fund for Nature has established an 'enterprise initiative' that seeks to involve schools in environmental problem solving. The oil company BP has published a 'Problem Solving with Plastics' pack. (See Appendix 2 for details of both.) All in all, these initiatives allow schools to begin to implement the problem-solving implicit and explicit in the National Curriculum in a number of ways.

PROBLEM-SOLVING AND EQUAL OPPORTUNITIES IN THE CURRICULUM

Before leaving problem-solving in the curriculum it is important to raise one vital concern: equal opportunities in the classroom. The first response one might make to an issue like this is: Can problem-solving in the curriculum really be sexist, racist or classist? In the normal course of events one might want to argue that this is impossible; surely scientific problems are neutral in the face of such things? But it is not difficult to appreciate that anything to do with society and its workings, with schools and schooling, and with industry and commerce, is prey to all the usual prejudices of life, and there is no reason to suppose that problem-solving in science and technology is any different.

Much has been made of the so-called neutrality or objectivity of science; its dispassionate, international nature. However, to repeat, societies around the world are riven by divisive biases of all sorts, and there is no reason to assume that science could ever be any different from, or somehow immune from, all this. Gill and Levidow (1987) make the case strongly that in some cases scientists not only perpetuate but actually generate prejudice and bias; their book looks at the implications of this for school science. Elsewhere (Nott and Watts, 1987; Watts, 1990), I have mourned the lost opportunities for policy-makers to tackle some of the issues at a national level, and even risked trying to suggest what a futuristic school science might look like (Bentley and Watts, 1986). But here let me spend a moment on specifics.

Mathews (1989) opens his article with a GIVEN problem:

> A racing track is 2.54 km long. A car goes round the track six times. How far has the car travelled?

He notes that in many trials of this question, boys did better than girls by 47% to 42%. When the question was rephrased as 'What is 2.54×6?' then girls outperformed boys and 64% got it right. He says:

> Suppose that every question given to a group of pupils referred to white men doing professional jobs. Boys who come from such a background have their lives validated, and hence can relate more easily to the questions. As the other extreme, a girl from an ethnic minority, whose parents are unemployed, would have more difficulty in relating to the questions.

This is clearly the case, too, with the type of problems that pupils might tackle in problem-solving activities. But what to do? For an 'even' approach we have to:

- Be always vigilant and critical of the biases and prejudices we might introduce ourselves, that would damage the sensitivities of others. None of us is without prejudice, and we must be constantly careful of what we say and how we act.
- Scrutinize materials for obvious signs of bias or imbalance so

that either these are used where the bias is highlighted as a teaching point or not used at all.

- Enable pupils wherever possible to OWN their problems. It is the case that problems will arise from pupils' own wants and needs, and tackling problems of this kind is to be encouraged; the notion of personal relevance in the ownership of problems and solutions is paramount.

- Encourage pupils where possible to solve problems through co-operative learning techniques. The most salient outcomes of research into co-operative learning point to the tremendous benefits for inter-group respect and esteem. There are good reasons for creating groups which are homogeneous in some respect — for example all-girl and all-boy groups. This can enable girls, say, to develop a particular way of working and raise specific issues for debate, effectively highlighting some of the different approaches women and men might take to solving a problem. However, as noted in Chapter 3, this is only one of several ways of developing groups.

These kinds of strategy will not solve all of society's problems at a stroke, of course, but they are short-, medium- and long-term measures aimed at resolving possible tensions. Some of the research underlying certain of the assumptions and statements I have been making is detailed in Chapter 6.

Chapter 6

Assessment, INSET and Research

INTRODUCTION

It may seem curious to leave the bulk of the traditional 'survey of literature' to the end of the book. While the other chapters are not entirely pragmatic in their approach, I have left some of the rationalization until the latter part of this chapter. Dealing with the 'heavy literature' in the very first chapter can sometimes be a daunting introduction, and yet the problem-solving ethos and process would be incomplete and uninformed without it. Here I start, though, with an introduction to assessment in problem-solving, and allow this to lead into a brief consideration of INSET (in-service education of teachers) provision in schools. The research issues come later.

ASSESSMENT

Assessment of problem-solving and open-ended project work is a long and complex issue, one not easily described in a few pages. At the time of writing the whole nature of assessment is changing almost daily: the Secretary of State for Education and the School Examinations and Assessment Council (SEAC) seem to publish a constant stream of directives. However, let me begin at both ends of a spectrum.

When problem-solving is an 'add-on' to the curriculum, as for instance a club activity, there is seldom need for formal assessment techniques. There is always need for *some* assessment and I return to examples of group and self-assessment in a moment. Where problem-solving is developed within a curriculum scheme, then there is usually a structured system for the assessment process built in. For example, some of the formalized CREST Project criteria have already been noted in Chapter 4; egg-race problem-solving comes complete with its own in-built rules and regulations; GCSE problem-solving is embroiled in its own sets of criteria and mark schemes. The Assessment of Performance Unit (for example Assessment of Performance Unit, 1984) provides a very sophisticated and well-analysed scheme for assessment in practical situations. The results are interesting and encompass many of the skills and processes listed in Chapter 2. In the middle of the spectrum, some difficulties can arise when schools wish to assess problem-solving and group-based activities that are not included in these kinds of initiative.

Over time there have been a number of attempts to set out techniques, strategies and processes of assessment, and it is worth discussing a few here. Most, though, eventually boil down to a check-list, commonly a check-list of skills or processes like those mentioned earlier. In this sense, assessment is usually fairly binary—a blank shows that the pupils did not (cannot) achieve that skill, a tick indicates that she or he has met some previously stated standard of attainment. An example of such a check-list is given by Hilton (1983), who illustrates a fairly usual list grouped under two main headings: 'observing and measuring' and 'planning and problem-solving'. The latter includes such processes as identifying a problem; suggesting explanations, causes, solutions; examining critically; implementing solutions and monitoring outcomes and so forth. As usual, the problems of trying to judge whether these criteria have been met are legion.

In her book, Di Bentley (1989) not only provides a range of check-lists for problem-solving at GCSE, but also discusses ways in which teachers can design and refine their own. A useful example for a GCSE format might, for instance, be that of the Northern Examining Board (Northern Examining Association, 1990) which set out its scheme for the assessment of groups of skills. So, for example, Skill 8 refers to 'being able to solve Technological Problems'. The rubric says:

> While engaged in tasks requiring the application of familiar science to the solution of simple technological problems, candidates should also be able to identify the parameters of the problem; devise a possible

solution to the problem; test and evaluate the proposed solution and if necessary repeat the whole process.

Solving technological problems requires candidates to use scientific ideas to offer solutions to problems which concern people or their environment. The expected differences between candidates might be in terms of the complexity of the problem, the level of scientific ideas used in the formulation of the solution and the quality of evaluation of those solutions.

The mark scheme that follows ranges from:

2 marks — 'can show rudimentary signs of achievement in the relevant skill'
6 marks — 'can identify a few factors associated with a problem; use simple scientific ideas in searching for a solution; with help, devise and test a single solution to a problem'

to:

10 marks — identify a wide range of factors associated with a problem, use the most appropriate scientific ideas to consider a range of possible solutions; devise and test a number of solutions, appreciating the need to repeat the procedure where necessary, to select the best taking full account of the original problem and the wider implications for society.

Clearly this kind of assessment is geared to a science syllabus rather than a technology one, and the marks and criteria are fairly broad and general. As Bentley (1989) points out, some GCSE schemes are very detailed with tightly defined criteria. Needless to say, both tight and loose criteria will appeal to different kinds of customer, and have their own benefits and drawbacks.

Self-Assessment

There are many forms of self-assessment and the suggestions here are by no means exhaustive. Easiest to use are forms similar to the CREST Criteria sheets such as the Gold sheet illustrated in Chapter 4, or the Bronze sheet shown here (Figure 6.1). These sheets have been used extensively and are the basis for the discussion between the problem-solver and the assessor. The intention is that the youngsters can understand what is required sufficiently to be able to describe the steps and outcomes of their work on at least two separate occasions.

CREST BRONZE AWARD
PROFILE OF PROBLEM-SOLVING SKILLS

You and your teacher will meet on at least two occasions to talk about your project At these meetings your progress will be assessed using the statements below. Each **goal or criterion** must be met on at least one occasion during the project. Of course, this does not apply if a particular criterion is not relevant to your investigation.

Name

Project Title

CREST Project Number _____ Individual ☐ Team ☐ Tick one

You can

Number of times assessed

	1	2	Optional			
Produce a workable idea/ideas in response to the problem set.						
Find out information to help you with your investigation.						
Select/reject possible ways of doing the investigation and explain your reasons.						
Design a fair test and predict what results you expect.						
Use your results to find out if they fit the idea being tested.						
Explain what your observations or results tell you in the light of what you are trying to find out.						
Attempt to cross check your results and explain the results that do not agree with the predictions you made.						
Alter and improve your investigation in the light of what you have found out.						
Work carefully and accurately.						
Record different ways of doing your investigation explaining the strengths and weaknesses of each approach.						
Record and explain why there may be more than one explanation for what you found out.						
Understand in what ways your experiment or prototype might not work in a different situation i.e. prototype uncertainty/accuracy limitation of experiments						
Explain how far you got in your CREST Award project, what problems you found and how you tried to overcome them.						

FINAL EVALUATION

The two sets of criteria are the goals which each student is meant to achieve during a project. It is the role of the Evaluator to make sure those goals are relevant to the project have actually been met.

The first set of criteria have been used by the group leader to complete the Profile of Problem-Solving Skills. The profile will be used when the Final Evaluation is made.

The Evaluator will decide whether the **second set of criteria** have been achieved at end of the project.

You should expect to

Explain clearly your part in planning and carrying out the project using your own words.

Demonstrate the fitness for purpose of the product of your work. Your log will help you do this.

Signature of Student _____ Date _____

Signature of Leader _____ Date _____

Signature of Evaluator _____

Date _____

Figure 6.1   Criteria of the CREST Bronze Award.

Where the process becomes 'bogged down', there is sometimes need for a kind of 'I'm stuck' chart, which, as the name implies, is a self-monitoring sheet for use when a stalemate is reached with the problem:

I am stuck/I'm not getting anywhere
I know . . .
Write down everything you know, or make notes on what you have done so far on the problem. Draw a picture, or a Concept Map (Spider diagram) of how the parts fit together so far.
I want . . .
Write the objective of the problem again in your own words. Also, write down any related questions that the problem suggests to you.
Try . . .
Write down some ideas. 'I wonder if . . .', 'Maybe . . .', 'What happens when I . . .?', 'What if I change . . .?'
Check . . .
Go back through your ideas. Try thinking about them as if you were explaining the problem to your younger sister or brother. Ask a friend to listen and be critical.

The next example is a check-list developed for use with youngsters at Key Stage 1, 2 and some of Stage 3. It is geared towards Attainment Target 10 in Science and so, in this case, is related to the topic of forces in physics. In this way it would be used as a 'content' self-assessment, for the youngster to judge his or her progress against the statements on the Levels of Attainment as laid down in the 'science document' (Department of Education and Science, 1989):

Pupil self-assessment in the National Curriculum Attainment Target 10: things I know about forces

Level 1
I know that things move if they are given a push by something or someone.

Level 2
I understand that if I push or pull things, they will move. If I push and pull harder or slower they will move faster or slow down and stop. If I push something from the side when it is going in a straight line, I can make it swerve.

Level 3
(a) I know that movement is caused by forces and that there are several different kinds of forces which act on things. These forces

make them move, stop, change direction, swerve or change shape.

(b)   I know that some things float in liquids and others sink. I understand that things float because there are forces in the liquid that are helping them to do so and that the forces helping them to float are greater than the forces pulling them down in the liquid.

Level 4

(a)   I can make a model that moves because it is powered by an elastic band or by the wind. From watching my model I can understand that it moves faster the greater the force that acts on it—if I wind the rubber band up tighter, for instance, or if the wind is very strong. It also changes direction depending on the forces acting on it.

(b)   I know that if a car or bicycle is going to go faster it needs a greater force pushing it. If it is going fast and needs to stop, it takes longer to stop if there is a large force acting on it than if there is only a little one.

(c)   I know that when I drop things they are attracted downwards towards the earth because of the force of gravity.

(d)   I know that my weight is really a measure of the force of gravity on me. I know that scientists measure this force in newtons, even though when I step on the scales I measure my weight in pounds or kilograms.

Level 5

(a)   I understand that something only changes direction or moves faster or more slowly because of the change in the balance of the forces that are acting on it. If something is standing still, it is because all the forces acting on it are balanced and no one is stronger than any other.

(b)   I have built a structure (such as a bridge) and tested it to see how strong it is, and I can tell somewhat what the weakest parts of its construction are.

(c)   I can measure forces and distances and time and I know what each of them is measured in. I can use instruments when I measure things to make my measurements as accurate as possible.

(d)   I know that cars can only travel and people can only walk in the way they do because of a force called friction. I understand that when there is very little friction—like at an ice rink—people move in different ways from what I am used to.

The list is (I hope) written in 'user-friendly' terms so that the pupils can look both at the criteria and at their own performance and, in so doing, assess their own progress. This version seems to work quite well although it is the result of a number of rewrites and could no doubt do with more.

A group assessment sheet

Below is an example of a group assessment sheet, where youngsters are asked to *jointly* respond to the following questions:

Question	*Comment*
1. Who was in your group?	
2. Did you all work well together?	
3. Did you discuss the problem *before* you started?	
4. Did you share out the work evenly?	
5. Did you all feel confident about designing your solution?	
6. Are you *happy* with what you have achieved?	
7. Did you write notes about what you were doing as you went along?	
8. Did you learn a lot from the research?	

This kind of list can meet a number of objectives. It clearly asks the group to reflect on their performance as a group, and to see what they might improve in future tasks. It also helps to isolate some of the skills in group work and, in line with comments made earlier about reinforcing feedback to groups, can be very important in highlighting the teacher's approval of positive group processes.

As I suggested earlier, these are just a few examples of what self- and group assessment sheets might look like. It is possible to design many different variations on these themes.

IN-SERVICE TRAINING AND PROBLEM-SOLVING

It is difficult to be precise in a world that changes as quickly as education does. On the whole, the on-the-job training of teachers depends largely on three general factors:

- individual and corporate training needs;
- the availability of suitable training provision;
- the money to fund it all.

Training needs are established in a number of ways: by government departments, local education authorities, school managers, head teachers, school departments and individuals in the system. As appraisal grows into a more common form of professional development, it will be linked more easily with individual INSET needs.

The suitability of provision depends upon a range of things, including: what the LEA can provide; the available university and institute courses; what the subject associations and professional bodies can offer. The money available for training remains another tangle of possibilities. In all of this, in-service work for problem-solving is usually a low priority. This is probably as it should be, since there are many other priority areas in education. However, for initiates, or the developing *aficionados*, there might be a need to gain further insights into what they want to do, and there have been some moves to make provision available.

The Association for Science Education holds its annual conference in January each year. It is a grand, national and multi-layered event and it is very unusual for a year to go by without some aspect of problem-solving appearing on the programme. The conference is open to non-members and the association's address is given in Appendix 2. Similarly, as already mentioned, the CREST Project is a national concern and the central office (see Appendix 2) can also provide some information of INSET provision. For example, CREST is currently working alongside the World Wide Fund for Nature to encourage both teachers and pupils into environmental problem-solving. General information can usually be obtained from a local university or institute of education. This is true, too, of many of the SATRO offices and their contact personnel and addresses are available through local education offices.

Most commonly, however, individual teachers will want to try things themselves, with their own pupils in the course of school activities. In this sense there is no other advice than to go ahead and do so; the best way to tackle problem-solving is to treat it as an activity in its own right. The teacher will be solving many organizational and managerial problems of an educational nature even as the pupils are solving problems technologically. The fun and enterprise of the occasions can (and has been) contagious, and developing solutions becomes a way of life at all sorts of levels. In this sense, I hope that some of the case studies of school activities in Chapter 5 will be of use for the beginner; further advice can be found in Bentley and Watts (1989).

PAST RESEARCH AND WAYS OF WORKING

In this section I want to begin with some general scene-setting and consider the research on problem-solving. The past has provided many important benchmarks for the way we might want to work today, but we have now to select from what we know, to use some parts of that knowledge and reject others.

The 'research stage' in the traditional problem-solving cycle or method is sometimes depicted as being one of the first stages, so that the research throws up a range of ideas or solutions, and helps to inform the design at the outset. I personally think that research is something that continues throughout the problem-solving activity, and informs the process all along the way. Reading around the topic, asking questions and listening to others does not stop even though some crucial decisions have already been made. No product or solution is ever the *final* say on the matter and there are always improvements, redesigns and alternative ways of working that could have been mounted. There is a well-known aphorism to the effect that it is only when you have arrived at a conclusion to the problem that you know how it *should* have been done.

I have delayed consideration of the research on problem-solving until this point in the book for the purpose of emphasizing my feelings about the non-linearity of the problem-solving process: given the nature of prose, books are often much more linear than real-life problems. First I begin with a broad background.

A BACKGROUND TO SCIENCE AND TECHNOLOGY EDUCATION

It has long been one of the central aims of education that youngsters should attain a basic understanding of the world we live in — and who would argue with that? In this context, the role of science in advanced technological societies, and the interaction between science, technology and society, have increasingly become an integral part of the school science curriculum. Over recent time, the key words in the development of the science and technology curriculum have been:

- breadth
- balance
- social and vocational relevance
- differentiation
- progression

To appreciate such terms is to look backwards over the last few years. For example, the Secondary Science Curriculum Review (1983) suggested that school science should provide opportunities for students to:

> use their knowledge of science to design and develop solutions to technological problems, to test and evaluate those solutions and to cost such exercises; and study key areas of science and technology that relate to the world of work and leisure so that they are better able to participate in a democratic society.

A little later the Department of Education and Science (1985) noted that few science courses draw on the experiences that pupils bring from their everyday lives. In classrooms, for instance, most experiments and many illustrative examples are laboratory based and divorced from the present world. Too many examples of the technological applications of science included in science courses and examinations reflect past developments rather than current ones. The Department said:

> science education should be presented and assessed in a way that allows the pupils to see the relevance to their lives; and it should draw on the environment and experience of the pupils themselves. One test for the inclusion of topics or approaches in a science course — and for the balance between physical and biological science — should be their value to pupils, of both sexes and all abilities, in their adult working lives in the world of the future.

As we know from the National Curriculum, such aims have now been elevated to policy and structured within Parliamentary orders. I noted in Chapter 1 that within the National Curriculum (Department of Education and Science, 1989) it is seen as important that pupils should be encouraged to study the application of science and the way it is changing our society. Pupils, says the DES, should be encouraged to explore some of the moral dilemmas that scientific discoveries can cause; should appreciate their responsibility as members of a society; and be given the confidence, through science education, to make a positive contribution to it.

This emphasis requires teachers to examine traditional teaching techniques within laboratories, and to explore new strategies through projects, investigations, simulations and role play, and ubiquitous coursework. This in turn raises a series of important questions about the nature of individual learning and participation in group work.

DIRECTIONS OF REFORM: PEDAGOGY

The HMI (1987) reported that science classes suffered from:

> deficiencies in course planning . . . [and] in the teaching styles and methodology. Even in schools where good practice was seen, there were examples of poor planning and enthusiasm for the subject. There was over reliance on works-cards and their use was not well planned . . . teachers talked for extended periods without recourse to class discussion. When discussion happened, it was often ill-disciplined and aimless . . . Pupils were rarely given the chance to plan their own investigations or even asked to suggest experiments.

The assumptions that underlie such a critique are that:

- traditional didactic methods of instruction are limited in achieving all curricular aims;
- such methods are ineffective with any other than highly motivated and achieving learners;
- a wide set of aims for science education allied to increasingly heterogeneous ability classroom groupings, requires a broad and flexible repertoire of teaching skills.

That is, didactic teaching encourages passive learning (Bentley and Watts, 1989), whereas balanced science for all requires the promotion of active learning (Dobson, 1987).

It is here that problem-solving begins to make an entry. Problem-solving has, for example, been an integral part of the framework for assessment developed by the Assessment of Performance Unit (Assessment of Performance Unit, 1984); it has headed the list of recommended teaching approaches in the Department of Education and Science's policy statement (Department of Education and Science, 1985); it has featured prominently in the work of the Secondary Science Curriculum Review (Secondary Science Curriculum Review, 1987a); is alive and well, as I have noted, in the rubric of the National Curriculum (Department of Education and Science, 1989); is firmly in the focus of technologically and vocationally orientated courses, from CPVE and CDT to maths and home economics (see, for example, Black and Harrison, 1985; Further Education Unit, 1986), and is now to be found as the subject of in-service seminars and conferences (Heaney and Watts, 1988; Watts and West, 1990).

I noted in Chapter 3 that the National Curriculum Working Party for Science (Department of Education and Science, 1988) frames its recommendations for science against the analogy between working scientists and children-as-scientists. The analogy suggests that children's development of scientific ideas parallels the development of scientific ideas in general. It is a child-centred approach, which sees an essential role for the teacher as 'enabler'. Rather than simply being an imparter of knowledge, the teacher 'may interact with the pupil, raise questions, build in appropriate challenges and experiences, and offer new ways of thinking'.

At policy level, the Department of Education and Science (Department of Education and Science, 1985) believes that adopting different teaching approaches to those currently used would be 'conducive to the success of the national policy objectives' defined in their policy statement. Changes are necessary, it argues, in order to encompass the ideals of broad and balanced science for all. It says:

> science teachers have much to gain from considering the implications for science of the variety of methods defined in paragraph 243 of the Cockcroft Report as desirable means for the more effective teaching of mathematics:
>
>> problem-solving;
>> investigation;
>> practical work;
>> exposition;
>> discussion, and
>> consolidation and practice.

Such a range of teaching approaches seems to the Department to be essential for the teaching of science as well as of mathematics; the key to success lies in flexibility and variety within such a repertoire. In particular, opportunities for pupils to contribute their own ideas to discussion are important, with the object of establishing that in science recourse to experiment and experimental data is the principal means of testing whether a hypothesis is supported by evidence, and if so how far its implications extend. The opportunities for pupils to engage in experimental work in which a variety of practical and investigative skills are developed under the supervision of the teacher is also of crucial importance. The balance in practical work should be more towards solving problems and less towards illustrating previously taught theory.

The reference to the Cockroft Report in the early part of the quote is somewhat misleading. Cockroft (1982) does indeed exhort mathematics teachers to consider a wide range of teaching approaches. The report, however, concedes in the very next paragraph that few mathematics teachers actually make use of such methods, nor is there very much research in mathematics education to support such moves.

INVESTIGATION AND PRACTICAL WORK

Recent surveys indicate that there is no lack of practical 'hands-on' activity in science lessons, particularly in the early years of secondary schooling. Lessons at this stage usually involve a high proportion of practical investigation. Beatty and Woolnough (1982), for example, surveyed 11-13 science and found that youngsters spend between 40% and 80% of their time doing practical work. As with problem-solving, though, investigation and practical work seems to fall into two camps. On the one hand is routine 'confirmatory' practice, which is geared to the rehearsal of known principles and laws. On the other hand is genuine investigation of phenomena and/or variables for which the answers or principles are only partially known and understood. This second kind of activity would appear to be at a premium.

Teachers in the Beatty and Woolnough survey, for instance, described four types of activity: 'standard exercises' (emphasizing particular procedures and developing skills in using them); 'teacher-directed discovery experiments'; 'demonstrations'; and 'project work'. Of these, the first two were the most common and the last the least common. This is reinforced by HMI reports, which state (Department of Education and Science, 1987):

> Practical work is undertaken but the work gives few opportunities for pupils to design investigations or interpret observations. The attention given to teaching practical skills is spasmodic and insufficient. Pupils start their courses with high expectations; they enjoy working in specialist rooms and being involved in practical work . . . However, the pupils seen were often more bewildered than enlightened by what they did. They were generally not challenged sufficiently by the work.

None of the teachers in Beatty and Woolnough's study highlighted features which deviate from standard didactic teaching; their description of youngsters' normal activities in class was 'teacher directed discovery experiments'.

In Science Education 5-16, the Department of Education and Science (1985) is quite clear about the purpose of practical activities in science:

> The Secretaries of State attach great importance to encouraging effective learning through extensive practical experience. In the first three secondary years the experience of scientific activity is still new and exciting to many pupils. Skilled teaching, well matched to the individual abilities of pupils can capitalise upon that sense of excitement and produce continuing enthusiasm for science.

One agreed purpose of practical experiences in the lower secondary school, then, is to encourage enthusiasm and excitement. The DES, however, does criticize present practice as fulfilling the function of 'illustrating previously taught theory' (Department of Education and Science, 1985, p. 18) rather than encouraging skills.

Practical work, then, is advocated to encourage skill development and enable youngsters to test out their ideas about science. That youngsters do gain from such approaches to teaching and learning is evidenced by classroom teachers such as Doherty (1989) when she says:

> pupils learnt new skills. For example, they learnt communication skills; planning and pacing; working to deadlines; competitive skill and working with the minimum of supervision. They all stated that they had enjoyed the work . . . and felt that in future they would like the project to be more open-ended.

In this sense GCSE coursework assessments could have a profound effect on practical work in both lower and upper school.

PS1 AND PS2 PROBLEM-SOLVING

Earlier chapters are testimony to the enormous variety in types of problems and, perhaps because of this, research into problem-solving has a long pedigree. In the 1970s and mid-1980s, the bulk of the literature referred to problems that are calculations or 'mental' problems in very much the arithmetic GIVEN mode, so that Newell and Simon (1972) in *Human Problem Solving*, for example, focus largely on mathematical problems, IQ games and the like. This research permeated science education primarily through chemistry (Ashmore *et al.*, 1979; Elliott, 1982; Black and Elliott, 1983) and physics (Clement 1979; Larkin *et al.*, 1980; Chi *et al.*, 1981), whether at high-school, A-level and early undergraduate study. In an article written jointly with John Gilbert (Watts and Gilbert, 1989) I have called problem-solving of this first kind Problem-Solving 1 (PS1) — it concerns the solution of well-defined GIVEN problems with little, if any, redundant information and with 'software' (paper-and-pencil) outcomes.

Problem-solving in the late 1980s (PS2), however, is different. As we have seen, problems can have software or 'hardware' solutions. They vary enormously and can range from puzzles and egg-races to design-and-make activities, extended project work, and 'real-world' problems. Throughout, there is usually a strong emphasis on skills, processes and a 'problem-solving method' or 'design process'. This is part of the growing tradition which has roots in the search for relevance in science, for applications of scientific principles and for technological education within science.

I have previously summarized the differences between PS1 and PS2 as follows:

PS1 concerns:
- problem-solving as a purely intellectual process;
- solving 'mental' or quantitative problems from textbooks — allied to an academic study of science and little or no overt 'technology';
- well-defined tasks, with little or no redundant information;
- the production of individual solution 'protocols' or routines;
- a focus on differences between the solution routines of novices and experts; for example, experts have been found to be four times faster than novices (Simon and Simon, 1978; Larkin, 1981) in reaching a correct solution;

- developing instructional strategies to enrich novices' representational structures and problem-solving repertoires, geared to increasing student intellectual skills and examination success;
- primarily an individualistic affair allied to didactic teaching.

The picture is one of developing and honing the intellectual skills of GIVEN mathematical problems.

On the other hand, PS2 concerns:

- problem-solving as an implementation task — translating concepts into practical outcome;
- largely qualitative, real-life, or curriculum-dedicated technological problems, allied to investigatory or practically based school science;
- ill-defined tasks, with only outline relevant information and materials supplied;
- the production of either a software *or* hardware solution, and usually a group solution, regardless of route;
- few references to expert solutions, except perhaps in final outcomes;
- a focus on developing problem-solving strategies which involve practical experimentation to develop cognitive, manipulative and affective skills;
- primarily a group activity allied to heuristic teaching, allied to project or coursework and 'active learning' approaches.

The traditional heavy emphasis on PS1 types of problem in science has thrown up conceptual difficulties for youngsters, and much of the research on concepts and conceptual change through problem-solving, noted in Chapter 3, began against a background of this kind — see, for example, Viennot (1979), Clement (1979) and Reif and Heller (1981). In some ways, consideration of youngsters' 'alternative conceptions' was a recognition of some of the drawbacks of didactic, mathematically based science teaching (Watts, 1988).

Current problem-solving (PS2) activities are quite different. There has, however, been little if any research into the nature of task-orientated technological problem-solving. Nevertheless, there are good reasons to suppose that PS2 problem-solving will survive the next few years. It is firmly embedded, for instance, in the rhetoric, if not the practice, of National Curriculum science. As a non-didactic method, problem-solving is highly rated. Just as importantly, it currently features in the coursework assessment for most GCSE boards. Throughout, the emphasis is on students tackling problems using a planned approach, with the appropriate technological processes and basic skills of scientific method as support.

PROBLEM-SOLVING AS A TEACHING STRATEGY

Problem-solving is founded on at least five major assumptions:

- First, as Kahney (1986) maintains, a person has a 'problem' when she or he has a goal that cannot be achieved directly, and activities (mental and/or physical) taken in pursuit of that goal can be regarded as problem-solving.
- Problem-solving involves the transfer of cognitive content and skills, of learning in one context affecting the learning of other material. In this sense, conceptual change and problem-solving have similarities in that they involve using already existing ideas and modifying them to fit new circumstances.

Bearing in mind what has been said in earlier chapters, transfer of learning is notoriously difficult. In the APU surveys, youngsters performed least well when asked to apply their understanding of concepts in science from one context to another (Assessment of Performance Unit, 1988). The more different the context, the less successful the transfer.

Transfer of learning involves understanding how material learned at one point in time affects the learning of other material. Experience in earlier tasks may either facilitate (positive transfer) or hinder (negative transfer) the solving of related material.

In the trivial sense, even deciphering the problem requires the use of prior knowledge so that the problem can be located in personal realms of understanding. If that were not the case the problem would be nonsensical. More importantly, the more ill-defined the problem, the more prior knowledge, understanding, skills and attitudes the solver must import from previous learning and experience.

- problem-solving clearly concerns constructing a mental model of what needs to take place, sometimes called 'the process of concretization'.
- Kahney (1986) also suggests, as noted in Chapter 3, that experience of one problem does not necessarily transfer to another problem of the same type unless (a) people are aware of the similarity,

and (b) the second problem is similar to the first. Problem-solvers are more sucessful when told two problems are similar (homomorphic). They improve at transferring learning from one situation to another when they are given guidance, and/or when the differences between problems are quite small.

- People's ability to plan ahead is limited, and it is sometimes simpler to help break down the problem into a series of sub-goals. This can have the adverse effect of sending the solver off onto idiosyncratic routes, losing sight of the main goal and of the steps from one sub-goal to another.

Within all of this, I believe that problem-solving as a teaching strategy has been seized upon largely uncritically. Attempts have been made to put it into some kind of context (Heaney and Watts, 1988), but on the whole it has been taken almost as an article of faith to be a remedy for inadequacies in other methods of teaching. There is some evidence that open-ended approaches like this can, where youngsters are tackling a range of examinations, interfere with traditional modes of testing and act to depress overall examination results (Fitzsimmons, 1988).

CHANGES IN THE CURRICULUM

The adoption of problem-solving activities in school science courses is happening quite slowly. Early work in schools (for example, by Mathews *et al.*, 1981) attempted to simulate and explore the roles of scientists 'doing' science. It is increasingly seen as a valuable way of providing more open learning situations where youngsters are less constrained by didactic teaching methods.

One particular growth area has been in the twilight zone between science and technology. Black and Harrison (1985), for example, see problem-solving as the main element in the area formed by the complementary overlap of the two fields. They see science and technology being resource areas — both conceptually and physically — to be drawn upon in the service of solving problems. From another direction, the officers of the Further Education Unit (1986) see problem-solving as a principal means of meeting many of the aims and objectives behind the Certificate of Pre-vocational Education (CPVE). They too wish to draw on the resources of science and technology:

One way of considering science and technology within the CPVE context is as 'real world' problem solving. To this end, students need to attain basic skills in the application of scientific method and technological processes to solving problems.

The kinds of problem they have in mind are clearly more open-ended and relevant to real-life situations than the others. In this sense, teachers are required to develop practical alternatives to teaching science and technology. The CPVE board, for example, suggests:

> Safety considerations mean that an appropriately trained teacher needs to be in attendance in laboratories and workshops, but it does not necessarily mean that all students should be doing the same thing at the same time. The concepts of 'open access' or 'drop-in centres' or 'resource bases' have been used, enabling students to visit the supervised laboratory or workshop as they wish.

CHANGING FASHIONS IN RESEARCH

As fashions change so do research preoccupations. Research into students' alternative conceptions, for example that of Driver and Easley (1978), Driver and Erickson (1983) and Gilbert and Watts (1983), took over from problem-solving in the late 1970s. As noted above, it succeeded in part as a reaction to the models of teaching and learning that formed the context for problem-solving at that time.

Much PS1 research has concerned the differences between students' and experts' 'solution protocols' as they solved problems — often associated, for example, with Newton's laws and mechanics. The strategies and techniques used by novice and expert show both quantitative and qualitative differences:

- Experts have been found to be four times faster than novices (Simon and Simon, 1978; Larkin, 1981) at reaching a correct solution. The pause times between the retrieval of equations or groups of equations were also quite different (Larkin, 1979): experts produced streams of equations without pausing while novices paused for most of the time.
- Experts seem to apply a prior analysis or 'scientific intuition' to the problem before actually starting to solve it. Where novices rely on their own intuition, however, they can create a false analysis.

- Experts made fewer meta-statements than novices, who made frequent comments on errors made, the physical meaning of the equations, or the overall direction in the course of solving the problem. This continuous commentary may be the novice voicing uncertainties that an expert does not share.
- Experts tend to work by producing equations that can be solved using the information given as part of the problem. The novice tends to start by generating an equation that contains the unknown to be found and working backwards (Simon and Simon, 1978). This may reflect the way in which the expert feels that the problem is soluble; the expert has built up a fundamental set of sub-routines for basic types of problem, and classifies the problem accordingly very quickly. This facility, say Chi *et al.* (1981), lies in the rich internal representation that the expert has generated.

ANALYSING PROBLEM-SOLVING

Traditional problems in the PS1 vein are usually presented with a few pages of illustrative material on a particular principle, plus a number of worked out solutions that illustrate the principle. Then, at the end of that text, a series of problems are presented. The mere fact that they are presented together is a strong clue that they are all somehow related and that the same sub-routines should be used, even though the surface features of the problems may differ. The hope is that the students will end up storing a general abstraction which represents an overall strategy for solving these types of problems.

Once an analogous problem has been recognized the solution must be translated into a solution for the target problem. Solvers may develop a series of partial solutions to the target problem. Successive partial solutions can serve as a framework for modifying the most recent partial solution to produce a new one.

On the other hand, hints are readily available in real-world problems of the PS2 type. Problem-solvers draw on vicariously acquired knowledge—through what they see other people doing. There is no such thing as 'copying' other people's work; imitation is a viable strategy, it is perfectly legitimate to look at how other people have solved (or are solving) the same (or similar) problems. Gagne (1970), for instance, says:

The results of using rules in problem solving are not confined to achieving a goal, satisfying as that may be for the thinker. When problem solution is achieved, something is also learned, in the sense that the individual's capability is more or less permanently changed. What emerges from problem solving is a higher order rule, which becomes part of the individual's repertory. The class of situation, when encountered again may be responded to with greater facility by means of recall and is no longer looked on as a problem. Problem solving, then, must definitely be considered a form of learning.

Problem-solving in one context must be seen as appropriate for use in another context. It is worth repeating Gilbert's quote (Gilbert, 1987) when she says of young people that:

> problem solving exercises must be directly and obviously applicable to any previous discoveries, or the children may be confused by the change of direction, discard the previous information as useless and give up any attempt to reason for themselves.

NEW DIRECTIONS IN RESEARCH

There is always a need for bigger, better, more detailed, more cogent, more far-reaching research in education, certainly in science education. In my view, problem-solving is under-researched and therefore deserves greater scrutiny. What might such research tackle? We need to:

- Undertake more case studies of problem-solving in action. This book contains only a few of the possible variations on problem-solving that can be (and have been) achieved in schools. These could be case studies from the teacher's point of view and from the pupils' perspectives. Good case studies make the joys and difficulties ring true for the reader, give a sense of what is possible and stimulate thoughts like 'Could I do that?'
- Dissect some of the skills and processes more thoroughly so that we know better what sorts of skills are most easily transferable, and which ones remain obdurate. Transfer continues to be a difficult concept to research in the rough-and-ready context of classroom activities — the bulk of research has taken place within carefully controlled experimental circumstances. And yet transfer remains the crux of the issue — it is because we want transfer of so-called 'generic skills' that we want to promote problem-solving in the first place.

- Delve more deeply into problem-solving and constructivism. Embedded within constructivism are some general principles of human learning, and these need to be clearly matched against some of the more overt principles underlying problem-solving. One interpretation of the work of Kelly (1955) is that life *is* problem-solving — people are engaged in a life-long quasi-scientific search for solutions to everyday problems.
- Institute longitudinal studies that allow us to monitor changes over a significant period of time. This is really a funding issue — it is seldom possible to call on research funding that permits a study of children over, say, a ten-year period. It is this kind of vertical slice on young people's developmental progress that would allow us to study such issues as transfer, the development of skills, the construction of world views and their negotiation within problem-solving situations. Good research might throw some light on the efficiency of problem-solving in the teaching of science concepts.
- Make claims about the long-term benefits of problem-solving, through problem-solving in life world situations. It could be argued that problem-solving is really tantamount to a series of decision-making tasks within a particular context. People make decisions on any number of grounds which may or may not bear any relationship to a 'problem-solving cycle'.
- Continue to broaden the contexts of problem-solving within the school curriculum, so that problem-solving within the environment, in industry and commerce, in medicine and health care, within information handling and computing, receive as much attention as problem-solving in mathematics and physics.

All in all, there seems to be a wealth of work yet to be done and many, many more problems to be solved.

Appendix 1: Further problems

In addition to the many lists and problems to be found within the book, here are further problems, variations and problem titles to begin a Problem Bank. They are in various stages of GIVEN and GOAL:

The bottle problem

Some drinks makers sell drinks in bottles that are returnable. They want to use the bottles again so as to keep the costs down. A returned bottle has to have the label removed, be cleaned, filled, relabelled and sent out again. Your job is to work as a research team to find the best glue for the labels. You have to plan and do an experiment to find the best glue. You have to give a report to the manager.

Studying woodlice

Here are some possible areas of investigation:

What living conditions do they like best?
How does their speed of movement change with temperature?
What do they eat and how do they feed?
Can they hear, see or smell?
How do they behave in a magnetic field?
Do the different species behave in the same way or differently?
Can they learn a simple thing like finding their way out of a maze?
Do they prefer to be together in groups, pairs or on their own?
What other things about woodlice do you think may be interesting to study?

A similar series of investigations can be undertaken with garden snails:

How can you make them move in the direction you want them to?
What surfaces do they prefer to travel on?

Periscope

Design and construct a periscope that enables you to look back over your
head. It must be portable and robust, and the final result must produce
an upright image.

Monocular

Design and build a monocular that is portable and robust and produces
an upright image. It must have a magnification of at least two, and be
less than 25 cm long.

Projector

Design and build a projector for a microscope slide. The system should
produce a real image at a distance of 1 to 1.5 m from the object. The
image should be at least 25 cm high but not more than 50 cm high. The
final system should be mounted on a base that is reasonably portable.
The projector may have a separate power supply and the system should
be designed so that the slides can be changed easily.

The desert island problem

You are shipwrecked on a desert island, with very minimal resources to
survive. In the laboratory you are allowed to use standard scientific
equipment to test your ideas, but you must say how you would put these
into practice on the island. You must find ways of:

producing some drinking water
making a shelter
disposing of waste
generating convenient heat
cooking
producing food
making and maintaining clothing.

Paper aeroplane

Design and make a paper aeroplane from a sheet of A4 paper
(210 mm × 295 mm). You must be able to land the plane on a target

diameter 1 m, which is 7 m from the point of launch.

Any of these parameters can be changed to make the problem easier or more difficult. The time limit can be constrained and additional materials (paperclips, Sellotape, Blu-Tack) can be allowed.

Dimmer switch

Many homes and theatres have dimmer switches to control the brightness of lights. Design one, with the materials available, to operate safely in a dolls' house.

Paper towels

Develop a 'fair test' for the absorbency of three different brands of paper kitchen towels.

Crude oil

Oil production sites are frequently in remote areas and so crude oil needs to be transported to a refinery for processing. Crude oil is very viscous and this can pose great difficulties in cold conditions (like those found in Alaska). How can it be transported safely and within budget?

Rubber seals

From the samples of rubber provided, choose one that would be best for an oil pump, to work in extreme conditions – for example, the North Pole and the Sahara.

Car crash

You are required to test the given materials for their suitability in car body design. The car body must be reasonably light but must be able to save the life of an occupant in the case of a crash.

Soft fruit

When soft fruits are frozen, ice crystals are formed. The crystal size is important because if they are too large they rupture the cells and spoil the fruit. Investigate the relationship between freezing time and crystal size for different soft fruits.

Grape sugar

Grapes are sometimes partly frozen to concentrate the sugar in the must prior to being crushed for fermentation. Investigate which temperature of freezing gives the highest sugar level on crushing.

Ball game

Invent a game in which a ball is used but which is very different to other ball games. There may be any number of players and the ball may be of any size you choose. You must design any other implements needed (nets, bats, goals, etc.).

Slow roller

In an industrial application a hollow steel tube is required to roll down a 45° inclined plane at a constant speed. It can be given an initial push and the tube can be sealed, but you must design only the minimum of constraints on the tube as it travels.

Floating egg

Make an egg float in liquid inside a jar so that the egg is 2 cm above the base of the jar. There should be no other mechanical means of support.

PROBLEM TITLES

What are the effects in the immediate environment of lead in petrol?
Design and make a small self-contained cooker that will cook one egg as quickly as possible.
Design and make a water salinity tester.
Design and make a survival beacon for use in the North Sea.
Design and make a small vehicle that will climb a slope of 1 m at 45°.
Use a '555' microchip timer to make a rain detector.
How can you reduce home electricity bills?
Make a device for a blind person so that the person can safely pour a cup of boiling water.

Design and construct a cat flap that will only allow your own pet cat to enter the house.

Investigate the polyunsaturated, mono-unsaturated and/or saturated fatty acid content of some common foods, such as semi-skimmed milk and margarine.

Produce a bacterial culture of a particular species, free from the presence of other micro-organisms.

Investigate the effects of common household chemicals on *Daphnia*.

Design an automatic brake that will gently slow a runaway wheelchair, pram or pushchair if it exceeds a certain speed.

Design a device for an old person to lift up a bottle of milk without having to bend over.

Develop an automatic greenhouse watering system to water the plants while you are away on holiday.

How to choose a microwave cooker?

Use a computer database to log your book or record collection.

Design a portable alarm system for both fire and security purposes.

Can moss be safely used as an emergency padding under a bandage over an open wound?

Survey the dietary and/or health issues in a local population.

Monitor and adjust soil conditions to maximize the growth of cress seeds.

Biocells—produce an electric current using a microbe such as yeast.

Design a shaker for flasks, or stirrer for beakers, in which microbes are grown in broth.

There are many, many more!

Appendix 2: Bibliography and sources of problems

This is an eclectic list of materials that have some bearing on problem-solving. Sometimes the sources listed are a fund of ideas; in other cases they concern more the whys and wherefores of problem-solving.

Association for Science Education, College Lane, Hatfield, Herts. AL 10 9AA.

Avon County Council (1986) *Problem Solving in Science 11–13*. Bristol: Resources for Learning Development Unit.

Ayeni, A. (1984) An investigation into the problem solving skills of high-school chemistry students. M.Sc. Thesis. Reading: University of Reading.

Barlex, D. and Kimbell, R. (1986) *CDT Projects and Approaches*. Basingstoke: Macmillan. Some good ideas and introduction to the design process.

Bell, B., Watts, D.M. and Ellington, E.C. (1985) *Learning, Understanding and Doing in Science*. Schools Curriculum Development Council, 45 Notting Hill Gate, London. A collection of conference papers on children's learning in science.

Bolton, W. (1977) *Physics Investigations*. Oxford: Pergamon Press.

Bowker, M.K., *et al.* (1986) *Problem Solving for the Less Able*. Available from M. Bowker, Worcester College of Higher Education, Worcester.

Brent Science (1988) *GCSE Revision Booklet*. Education Offices, London Borough of Brent. Contains some good examples of open-ended work.

British Association (1984) *Ideas for Egg Races and Other Practical Problem Solving Activities*. Compiled by the British Association for the Advancement of Science, London.

British Petroleum (1989) *Problem Solving with Plastics*. London: BP Educational Service. A comprehensive folder of industrially related problems.

Carlin, P. and Fearn, F. (1988) *Everyday Science*. Available from F. Fearn, Littlemoss High School, Cryer Street, Droylsden, Manchester.

County of Hereford and Worcester (1986) *Problem Solving for the Less Able*. Education Offices, County of Hereford and Worcester.

CREST Project. Details available from: Alan West, CREST Project, Fortress

House, 23 Savile Row, London Wl; or through Education Liaison Centre, University of Surrey, Guildford, Surrey. CREST is a national award scheme for problem-solving in the secondary age range. It has a comprehensive database of problems.

EARO (1985) *Problem Solving: Does It Work?* East Anglia Resource Organisation, Back Hill, Ely, Cambridgeshire. A package of five videos and background papers on problem-solving in key stages 1–4.

Engineering Council (1985) *Problem Solving: Science and Technology in Primary Schools.* London: Engineering Council and SCSST.

Evans, R.J., *et al.* (1988) *Problems, Problems!* Available from M. Holmes, Wern Teachers' Centre, Sebastopol, Pontypool, Gwent.

Further Education Unit (1982) *Basic Skills.* London: Further Education Curriculum Review and Development Unit, Department of Education and Science.

Further Education Unit (1986) *Supporting Science and Technology in CPVE.* London: Further Education Unit.

Garrett, R.M. (1986) Problem-solving in science education. *Studies in Science Education*, **13**, 70–95.

Gowers, P. (1987) *Design and Communication for Foundation Courses.* Glasgow: Blackie.

Graham, H.R. (1988) *Medical Technology.* Available from the Association for Science Education (North East Region), 50 Davison Avenue, Whitley Bay, Tyne and Wear. Some useful problems and contexts from the world of medicine and hospitals.

Heaney, J. and Watts, D.M. (1988) *Problem Solving: Ideas and Approaches from the Secondary Science Curriculum Review.* York: Longman, for the Schools Curriculum Development Committee.

Hopson, B. (1984) *Teaching Lifeskills.* London: Harper & Row.

Howlett, A., *et al.* (1986) *The Desert Island Problems.* Peterborough Education Development Centre, Cottesmore Close, Westwood, Peterborough.

Industrial Archaeology Working Group (1989) *Industrial Archaeology.* Association for Science Education, Hatfield, Hertfordshire. A range of problems derived from geographical, archaeological and historical contexts.

Ingleby, D., Winspear, L. *et al.* (1987) *Biotech.* Hatfield: Association for Science Education. Some excellent problems and guidance in biotechnology.

Johnsey, R. (1986) *Problem Solving in School Science.* London: Macdonald Educational.

Leat, C., *et al.* (1986) *Links: Problem Solving Guidelines and Activities.* Available from Northants Science Centre, c/o Spencer Middle School, Lewis Rd, Northampton.

Linnell, H.D. and Gibson, D. (1987) *Problem Solving for the Less Able: 14–16 Age Group.* Available from: P. Cannon, Stockport Teachers' Centre, The Dialstone Centre, Lisburne Lane, Offerton, Stockport.

London Biotechnology Centre. South Bank Polytechnic, Borough Road, London SEl. The centre has a wealth of problems and resource material for work in biotechnology.

Millard, A., *et al.* (1986) *Biotechnology: A Teacher Sourcebook of*

Experiments and Evaluations of Curriculum Materials. Wiltshire Education Department, County Hall, Trowbridge, Wiltshire.

National Centre for School Biotechnology. Faculty of Education, University of Reading, Whiteknights, Reading.

Nicholls, L. (1986) *Problem Solving: A Teachers' Source Book.* Wiltshire Education Department, County Hall, Trowbridge, Wiltshire.

Olejnik, I. and Farmer, B. (1989) *Biology and Industry: Practical Biotechnology for A level.* Glasgow: Blackie.

Page, R., Clarke, R. and Poole, J. (1982) *Problem Solving: Schools Council Modular Courses in Technology.* Oliver & Boyd, in association with the National Centre for School Technology.

PEEL Seeds: The Newsletter of the PEEL Collective. Available from Ian Mitchell, Laverton Secondary School, PO Box 243, Laverton, Western Australia 3028.

Robertson, S., Dredge, A. and Coyle, P. (1988) *The Investigator.* Curriculum Council for Wales, Womanby Street, Cardiff.

Sage, J., *et al.* (1986) *Problem Solving in Science 11–13.* Resources for Learning Development Unit, Bishop Rd, Bishopston, Bristol.

SATIS: Science and Technology In Society (1983) Association for Science Education, Hatfield, Herts.

Surrey Biotechnology Bus. Details from Ann Riggs, Department of Educational Studies, University of Surrey, Guildford, Surrey. A mobile laboratory with excellent facilities for practical work in biotechnology.

Surrey SATRO. Department of Educational Studies, University of Surrey, Guildford, Surrey. The SATRO has a wealth of information and resource material on a variety of school/industry links and initiatives.

Swift, D.G., *et al.* (1986) *Problem Solving for Science Classes.* Department of Education, Huddersfield Polytechnic, Queensgate, Huddersfield.

Terrey, K., Parker, C. and Piper, A. (1986) *Microbiology/Biotechnology.* Isle of Wight County Council. Available from: the Teachers' Centre, Upper James St., Newport, Isle of Wight.

Wallman, R. (1985) *Problem Solving in Middle School Science.* M.A. thesis, University of London (KQC).

West, A. and Watts, D.M. (1988) *Working Together: A Joint TVEE/ Industry/SATRO venture. Issues from a Problem Solving Day.* CREST, University of Surrey, School of Education, Roehampton Institute, London.

West Yorkshire Applications Group (1986) *Problem Solving for Science Classes* (Mimeograph). Department of Education, Huddersfield Polytechnic.

Whitcombe, P.D. and Jones, B.D. (1988) *Problem Solving in Lower School Science.* Curriculum Council for Wales, Castle Buildings, Womanby Street, Cardiff.

White, N. and Bentley, D. (1987) *Chips with Everything.* Available from: N. White, Delhasfield, Greenscoe, Askam in Furness, Cumbria. Problem-solving through health education.

Williams, P. and Jinks, D. (1985) *Design and Technology 5–12.* Brighton: Falmer Press.

World Wide Fund for Nature. Details of the Fund's Environmental Enterprise Award are available from the World Wide Fund for Nature, Panda House, Weyside Park, Catteshall Lane, Godalming, Surrey GU7 1XR. Young Investigators Scheme. Further information available from: British Association for the Advancement of Science, Fortress House, 23 Savile Row, London Wl; or through Education Liaison Centre, University of Surrey, Guildford, Surrey.

References

Adey, P., Bliss, J., Head, J. and Shayer, M. (1989) *Adolescent Development and School Science*. London: Falmer Press.

Arieti, S. (1976) *Creativity: The Magic Synthesis*. New York: Basic Books.

Ashmore, A.D., Frazer, M.J. and Casey, R.J. (1979) Problem solving networks in chemistry. *Journal of Chemical Education*, 56 (6), 377–79.

Assessment of Performance Unit (1984) *Science in Schools: Age 13. Report No. 2*. London: HMSO.

Assessment of Performance Unit (1988) *Science at Age 15: A Review of APU Survey Findings 1980–84*. London: HMSO.

Baird, J.R. and Mitchell, I.J. (1986) *Improving the Quality of Teaching and Learning: An Australian case-study—the PEEL Project*. Melbourne: Monash University Printery.

Baldwin, J. and Williams, H. (1988) *Active Learning: A Trainer's Guide*. Oxford: Basil Blackwell.

Barnes, D. (1976) *From Communication to Curriculum*. Harmondsworth: Penguin.

Beatty, J.W. and Woolnough, B. (1982) Why do practical work in 11–13 science? *School Science Review*, 63 (225), 768–70.

Bentley, D. (1989) *GCSE Coursework: Science. A Teachers' Guide to Organisation and Assessment*. Basingstoke: Macmillan.

Bentley, D. and Watts, D.M. (1986) Courting the positive virtues: a case for feminist science. *European Journal of Science Education*, 8 (2), 121–34.

Bentley, D. and Watts, D.M. (1989) *Learning and Teaching in School Science: Practical Alternatives*. Milton Keynes: Open University Press.

Bentley, D. and Watts, D.M. (1990) *Communicating in School Science*. London: Falmer Press (in press).

Beswick, N. (1987) *Re-thinking Active Learning 8–16*. London: Falmer Press.

Black, P. and Elliott, H.G. (1983) Problem solving by chemistry students. In: Bliss, J., Monk, M. and Ogborn, J. (eds.) *Qualitative Data Analysis for Educational Research*. London: Croom Helm.

Black, P. and Harrison, G. (1985) *In Place of Confusion: Technology and*

Science in the School Curriculum. London and Trent: Nuffield-Chelsea Trust and NCST.

Brent, London Borough (1989) *I can do that! Brent Primary Science*. London: Education Department, London Borough of Brent.

Brook, A. and Wells, P. (1988) Conserving the circus? An alternative approach to teaching and learning about energy. *Physics Education*, **23** (2), 80–85.

Bruner, J. (1961) *The Process of Education*. New York: Vintage.

Burden, M., Emsley, M. and Constable, H. (1988) Encouraging progress in collaborative group work. *Education*, **3** (13), March, 51–56.

Chi, M.T.H., Feltovitch, P. and Glaser, R. (1981) Categorisation and representation of physics problems by experts and novices. *Cognitive Science*, **5**, 121–53.

Children's Learning In Science (CLIS) (1987) *Teaching Schemes*. Leeds: Centre for Science and Maths Education, University of Leeds.

Clement, J. (1979) Mapping a student's causal conceptions from a problem solving approach. In: Lochhead, J. and Clement, J. (eds.) *Cognitive Process Instruction*. Philadelphia: Franklin Institute Press.

Clough, E.E. and Driver, R. (1985) Secondary students' conceptions of the conduction of heat: bringing together scientific and personal views. *Physics Education*, **20** (4), 176–82.

Cockroft Report (1982) *Mathematics Counts: The Report of the Committee of Inquiry into the Teaching of Mathematics in Schools*. London: HMSO.

de Benedictis, T. (1980) *Observations of Problem Solving in Naturalistic Situations: Pilot Study to Determine a Methodology*. Mimeograph, Adolescent Reasoning Project (ARP) Report No. 23. Berkeley: Lawrence Hall of Science, University of California.

Department of Education and Science (1985) *Science 5–16: A Statement of Policy*. London: HMSO.

Department of Education and Science (1987) *The National Curriculum Science Working Party Interim Report*. London: HMSO.

Department of Education and Science (1988) *Science for Ages 5 to 16: The Report of the National Curriculum Science Working Group*. London: HMSO.

Department of Education and Science (1989) *Science in the National Curriculum*. London: HMSO.

Dobson, K. (1987) *Teaching for Active Learning: Coordinated Science Teachers' Guide*. London: Collins Educational.

Doherty, M. (1989) Teaching physics in an all-girls school, and ways of personalising their learning. In: Bentley, D. and Watts, D.M. (eds.) (1989) *Learning and Teaching in School Science: Practical Alternatives*. Milton Keynes: Open University Press.

Driver, R. (1988) A constructivist approach to curriculum development. In: Fensham, P. (ed.) *Development and Dilemmas in Science Education*. London: Falmer Press.

Driver, R. and Easley, J.A. (1978) Pupils and paradigms – a review of literature related to concept development in adolescent science students. *Studies in Science Education*, **5**, 61–84.

Driver, R. and Erickson, G.L. (1983) Theories-in-action: some theoretical and empirical issues in the study of students' conceptual frameworks in science. *Studies in Science Education*, **10**, 37-60.

Driver, R., Guesne, E. and Tiberghien, A. (1985) *Children's Ideas in Science.* Milton Keynes: Open University Press.

Driver, R. and Watts, D.M. (1990) Research on Students' Conceptions in Science: a Bibliography. Children's Learning in Science Research Group, University of Leeds.

Ellington, K. (1987) *Better Science, Curriculum Guide 4: Approaches to Teaching and Learning.* London: Heinemann Educational and Association for Science Education for Secondary Science Curriculum Review and Schools Curriculum Development Committee.

Elliott, H.G. (1982) Links and nodes in problem solving. *Journal of Chemical Education*, **59** (9), 719-20.

Engineering Council (1985) *Problem Solving: Science and Technology in Primary Schools.* London: Engineering Council and SCSST.

Fensham, P. (ed.) (1988) *Development and Dilemmas in Science Education.* London: The Falmer Press.

Fisher, R. (1987) *Problem Solving in Primary Schools.* Oxford: Basil Blackwell.

Fitzsimmons, C. (1988) Evaluating TVEI. Paper presented to the British Educational Research Association Annual Conference. School of Education, University of Newcastle on Tyne.

Foster, S. (1989) Streetwise physics. *School Science Review*, **70** (254), 15-25.

Furnham, A.F. (1988) *Lay Theories: Everyday Understanding of Problems in the Social Sciences.* Oxford: Pergamon Press.

Further Education Unit (1982) *Basic Skills.* London: Further Education Curriculum Review and Development Unit, Department of Education and Science.

Further Education Unit (1986) *Supporting Science and Technology in CPVE.* London: Further Education Unit.

Gagne, R.M. (1970) *The Conditions of Learning.* London: Holt-Saunders.

Gick, M.L. and Hoylake, K.J. (1980) Analogical problem solving. *Cognitive Psychology*, **12**, 306-55.

Gilbert, N.S. (1987) Solving problems in science. *Education*, **3** (13), 21-24.

Gilbert, J.K. and Watts, D.M. (1983) Concepts, misconceptions and alternative conceptions: changing perspectives in science education. *Studies in Science Education*, **10**, 61-91.

Gill, D. and Levidow, L. (1987) *Anti-Racist Science Teaching.* London: Free Association Press.

Greene, J. (1975) *Basic Cognitive Processes.* Milton Keynes: Open University Press.

Gunstone, R. and Watts, D.M. (1985) Children's ideas about force and motion. In: Driver, R. Guesne, E. and Tiberghien, A. (eds.) *Children's Ideas about Some Scientific Phenomena.* Milton Keynes: Open University Press.

Hadfield, J.M. (1987) Problem oriented structured teaching. *Education in Chemistry*, March, 43-44.

Hawking, S. (1988) *A Brief History of Time*. London: Bantam Press.

Heaney, J. and Watts, D.M. (1988) *Problem Solving: Ideas and Approaches From the Secondary Science Curriculum Review*. Harlow: Longman, for Schools Curriculum Development Committee.

Henriques, J., Holloway, W., Urwin, C., Venn, C. and Walkerdine, V. (1984) *Changing the Subject*. London: Methuen.

Hilton, B. (1983) Towards a skill based science curriculum. *Education*, 2, December, 457-9.

HMI (1987) *Report by HM Inspectors on Survey in Years 1-3 of Some Secondary Schools in Greenwich*. London: DES.

Hofstader, D.R. (1985) *Metamagical Themas: Questing for the Essence of Mind and Pattern*. Harmondsworth: Penguin Books.

Hudson, J., Millband, C. and Slack, D. (1987) *Science Horizons*. Basingstoke: Macmillan Educational.

Inner London Education Authority (1988a) *Science in Process*. London: Heinemann Educational and Inner London Education Authority.

Inner London Education Authority (1988b) *Helping Children to Become Scientific: Primary Science Guidelines*. London: Inner London Science Teachers Centre: South.

Institute of Manpower Studies (1982) *Skills Needed for Young People's Jobs: Some Applications of the Findings*. Brighton: Institute of Manpower Studies, University of Sussex.

Jackson, K.F. (1983) *The Art of Solving Problems: Bulmershe-Comino Problem-Solving Project*. Reading: Bulmershe College.

Johnsey, R. (1986) *Problem Solving in School Science*. London: Macdonald Educational.

Johnson, D.W., Johnson, R.T. and Scott, L. (1978) The effects of cooperative and individualised instruction on student attitudes and achievement. *Journal of Social Psychology*, 104, 207-16.

Johnson, D.W., Johnson, R.T. and Skon, L. (1979) Student achievement on different types of tasks under cooperative, competitive and individualistic conditions. *Contemporary Educational Psychology*, 4, 99-106.

Johnson-Laird, P.N. (1983) *Mental Models*. Cambridge: Cambridge University Press.

Kahney, H. (1986) *Problem Solving: A Cognitive Approach*. Milton Keynes: Open University Press.

Kelly, G.A. (1955) *The Psychology of Personal Constructs*, Vols. 1 and 2. New York: W.W. Norton.

Kutnik, P. and Thomas, M. (1989) Dyadic pairings for the enhancement of cognitive development in the science curriculum: some preliminary results. Paper presented to the British Educational Research Association Annual Conference, Newcastle upon Tyne. School of Education, University of Sussex.

Larkin, J.H. (1979) Processing information for effective problem solving. *Engineering Education*, 79 (3), 285-88.

Larkin, J.H. (1981) Enriching formal knowledge: a model for learning to solve textbook physics problems. In: Anderson, J. (ed.) *Cognitive Skills and Their Acquisition*. Hillsdale N.J.: Lawrence Erlbaum Associates.

Larkin, J.H., McDermott, J., Simon, D.P.T. and Simon, H.A. (1980) Models of competence in solving physics problems. *Cognitive Science*, **4**, 307–45.

Lovejoy, S. (1988) How to ZAP your problems: a problem solving technique for psychologists and teachers. *Educational Psychology in Practice*, **3** (4), January.

Mahoney, M.J. (1988) Constructive meta-theory. *International Journal of Personal Construct Psychology*, **1** (1), 1–36.

Mathews, B. (1989) Chaining the brain: structural discriminations in testing. In: Cole, M. (ed.) *The Social Context of Schooling*. London: Falmer Press.

Mathews, B., Schollar, J. and Hinton, K. (1981) *Problem Solving: Teachers' Guide* (Mimeograph). London: Roan School, Clissold Park School.

McKeachie, W.J. (1987) Cognitive skills and their transfer: discussion. *International Journal of Educational Research*, **11** (6), 707–12.

Miller, A.I. (1986) *Imagery in Scientific Thought*. London: MIT Press.

Miller, R. (1989) *Doing Science: Images of Science in Science Education*. London: Falmer Press.

Minstrell, J. (1982) Explaining the 'at rest' conditions of an object. *Physics Teacher*, 109–14.

Munson, P. (1988) Some thoughts on problem solving. In: Heaney, J. and Watts, D.M. (eds.) *Problem Solving: Ideas and Approaches from the Secondary Science Curriculum Review*. Harlow: Longman for Schools Curriculum Development Committee.

Murphy, P. (1988) Insights into pupils' responses to practical investigations from the APU. *Physics Education*, **23**, 331–6.

National Curriculum Council (1989a) *Science Non-Statutory Guidance*. York: National Curriculum Council.

National Curriculum Council (1989b) *National Curriculum Council Consultation Report: Technology*. York: National Curriculum Council.

Newell, A. and Simon, H.A. (1972) *Human Problem Solving*. Englewood Cliffs, New Jersey: Prentice-Hall.

Northern Examining Association (1990) *GCSE Science (Modular) Syllabus for the 1991 Examination*. Manchester: Northern Examining Association.

Nott, M. and Watts, D.M. (1987) Towards a multicultural and anti-racist science policy. *Education in Science*, **121**, January, 37–8.

Novak, J. (1985) Metalearning and metaknowledge strategies to help students learn how to learn. In: West, L.T. and Pines, A.L. *Cognitive Structure and Conceptual Change*. London: Academic Press.

Nussbaum, J. and Novick, S. (1981) Brainstorming in the classroom to invent a model: a case study. *School Science Review*, **62** (221), 771–8.

Osborne, R. and Freyberg, P. (1985) *Learning in Science*. London: Heinemann Educational.

Page, R., Clarke, R. and Poole, J. (1982) *Problem Solving: Schools Council Modular Courses in Technology*. Edinburgh: Oliver & Boyd, in association with the National Centre for School Technology.

Peacock, A. (1986) *Science Skills: A Problem Solving Activities Book*. Basingstoke: Macmillan.

Pfundt, H. and Duit, R. (1988) *Bibliography: Students' Alternative Frameworks and Science Education*. 2nd edn. IPN Reports in Brief, Kiel, Federal Republic of Germany: University of Kiel.

Pope, M.L. and Watts, D.M. (1988) Constructivist goggles: implications for process in teaching and learning physics. *European Journal of Physics*, 9, 101-9.

Reif, F. and Heller, J.I. (1981) Knowledge structures and problem solving in physics. In: *Proceedings of an International Workshop on Problems Concerning Students' Representation of Physics and Chemistry Knowledge*. Pädagogische Hochschule Ludwigsberg, Ludwigsberg, Federal Republic of Germany.

Rowlands, D. (1987) *Teachers' Manual: Problem Solving in Science and Technology*. Manchester: Manchester City Council Education Department.

Salomon, G. and Globerson, T. (1987) Skill may not be enough: the role of mindfulness in learning and transfer. *International Journal of Educational Research*, 11 (6), 623-37.

SATIS: Science and Technology In Society (1983) Hatfield: Association for Science Education.

Screen, P. (1986) *Warwick Process Science*. Southampton: Ashford Press.

Secondary Science Curriculum Review (1983) *Science 11-16. Proposals for Action and Consultation*. London: Secondary Science Curriculum Review; Schools Curriculum Development Committee.

Secondary Science Curriculum Review (1987a) *Better Science: A Directory of Resources*. London: Heinemann Educational and Association for Science Education, for Secondary Science Curriculum Review and Schools Curriculum Development Committee.

Secondary Science Curriculum Review (1987b) *Better Science: Choosing Content*. London: Heinemann Educational and Association for Science Education, for Secondary Science Curriculum Review and Schools Curriculum Development Committee.

Shapiro, B.L. (1988) What children bring to light. In: Fensham, P. (ed.) *Development and Dilemmas in Science Education*. London: Falmer Press.

Sharan, S. (1980) Cooperative learning in small groups: recent methods and effects on achievement, attitudes and ethnic relations. *Review of Educational Research*, 50 (2), 241-71.

Shayer, M. (1989) Hewers of wood and drawers of water? Or populations in change? In: Adey, P., Bliss, J., Head, J. and Shayer, M. (eds.) *Adolescent Development and School Science*. London: Falmer Press.

Shipstone, D. (1988) Pupils' understanding of simple electrical circuits. *Physics Education*, 23 (2), 92-6.

Simon, D.P.T. and Simon, H.A. (1978) Individual differences in solving physics problems. In: Siegler, R. (ed.) *Children's Thinking: What Develops?* Hillsdale, New Jersey: Lawrence Erlbaum Associates.

Slavin, R.T. (1978) Student teams and achievement divisions. *Journal of Research and Development in Education*, 12 (1), 39-49.

Solomon, J. (1985) Teaching the conservation of energy. *Physics Education*, 20 (4), 165-70.

Sparkes, D. and Soper, R. (1988) *Practical Assessment for GCSE Biology.* Cambridge: Cambridge University Press.

Stewart, D. (1987) *Better Science, Curriculum Guide 5: Making It Relevant To Young People.* London: Heinemann Educational and Association for Science Education, for Secondary Science Curriculum Review and Schools Curriculum Development Committee.

Strike, K.A. and Posner, G.J. (1985) A conceptual change view of learning and understanding. In: West, L.T. and Pines, A.L. (eds) *Cognitive Structure and Conceptual Change.* London: Academic Press.

Summers, M. and Kruger, C.J. (1989) An investigation of some primary teachers' understanding of change in materials. *School Science Review,* **71** (255), 17–27.

Surrey SATRO (1989) *Egg-Race Factfile.* Guildford: Surrey SATRO, University of Surrey.

Terry, C., Jones, G. and Hurford, W. (1985) Children's conceptual understanding of forces and equilibrium. *Physics Education,* **20** (4), 162–5.

Viennot, L. (1979) Spontaneous learning in elementary dynamics. *European Journal of Science Education,* **1** (2), 205–21.

Wallwork, D. (1989) Solving problems – relevance and creativity in science. In: Bentley, D. and Watts, D.M. (eds.) *Learning and Teaching in School Science: Practical Alternatives.* Milton Keynes: Open University Press.

Watts, D.M. (1983) *A Study of Alternative Frameworks in School Science.* Ph.D. thesis. Guildford: University of Surrey.

Watts, D.M. (1985) Student conceptions of light: a case study. *Physics Education* **20** (4), 183–7.

Watts, D.M. (1988) From concept maps to curriculum signposts. *Physics Education* **23** (2), 74–9.

Watts, D.M. (1990) Multicultural and anti-racist science – lost opportunities in policy making. In: Peacock, A. (ed.) *Multicultural Primary Science.* Basingstoke: Macmillan Educational (in press).

Watts, D.M. and Bentley, D. (1986) Methodological congruity in principle and in practice: a dilemma in science education. *Journal of Curriculum Studies,* **18** (2), 167–75.

Watts, D.M. and Gilbert, J.K. (1989) The new learning: research development and school science education. *Studies in Science Education,* **16**, 75–121.

Watts, D.M. and Michell, M. (1987) *Better Science, Curriculum Guide 2: Choosing Content.* London: Heinemann Educational and Association for Science Education, for Secondary Science Curriculum Review and Schools Curriculum Development Committee.

Watts, D.M. and Pope, M.L. (1989) Thinking about thinking, learning about learning: constructivism in physics education. *Physics Education,* **24**, 326–31.

Watts, D.M. and West, A. (1990) Problem solving in chemistry: a recipe for disaster? Submitted to *Education in Chemistry.*

West, A. (1988) CREST – awards for Creativity in Science and Technology. In: Heaney, J. and Watts, D.M. (eds.) *Problem Solving: Ideas and Approaches from the Secondary Science Curriculum Review.* Harlow: Longman, for Schools Curriculum Development Committee.

White, R.T. (1988) *Learning in Science*, Oxford: Basil Blackwell.
White, S. (1990) What children understand about heat and how this relates to the National Curriculum. In: Barber, B. and Watts, D.M. (eds.) *Doing the Difficult Bits*. An Occasional Publication from Roehampton Institute, London (in press).
Williams, P. and Jinks, D. (1985) *Design and Technology 5-12*, Brighton: Falmer Press.

Name Index

Adey, P. 54
Arieti, S. 81
Ashmore, A.D. 131
Assessment of Performance Unit
    (APU) 29, 30, 118, 128, 132

Baird, J.R. 76
Baldwin, J. 4
Barnes, D. 65
Beatty, J.W. 129-30
Bentley, D. 4, 8, 16, 33, 66, 68, 71,
    91, 96, 115, 118, 119, 125, 127
Beswick, N. 4
Black, P. 19, 22, 128, 131, 134
Bliss, J. 54
Brook, A. 55
Bruner, J. 7
Burden, M. 72

Casey, R.J. 131
Chi, M.T.H. 131, 136
Children's Learning in Science (CLIS)
    54, 60
Clarke, R. 29
Clement, J. 131, 132
Clough, E. 55
Cockroft Report 129
Constable, H. 72

de Benedictis, T. 124
Department of Education and Science
    (DES) 17, 42, 60, 61, 121, 126,
    127, 128, 129, 130

Dobson, K. 4, 127
Doherty, M. 130
Driver, R. 54, 55, 63, 135
Duit, R. 54

Easley, J. 54, 135
Ellington, K. 33
Elliott, H.G. 131
Emsley, M. 72
Engineering Council 8
Erickson, G. 135

Feltovitch, P. 131, 136
Fensham, P. 34
Fisher, R. 22, 81
Fitzsimmons, C. 134
Foster, S. 3
Frazer, M.J. 131
Freyberg, P. 54, 64
Furnham, A.F. 55
Further Education Unit (FEU) 13, 17,
    40, 78, 128, 134

Gagne, R. 7, 40, 136-7
Gick, M.L. 78
Gilbert, J.K. 131
Gilbert, N.S. 37, 38, 137
Gill, D. 115
Glaser, R. 131, 136
Globerson, T. 76
Greene, J. 9
Gunstone, R. 76

Hadfield, J.M. 38
Harrison, G. 19, 22, 128, 134
Hawking, S. 31
Head, J. 54
Heaney, J. 22, 128, 134
Heller, J.I. 132
Henriques, J. 65
Her Majesty's Inspectors (HMI) 127, 129
Hilton, B. 118
Hofstader, D.R. 80, 81
Holloway, W. 65
Hoylake, K.J. 78
Hudson, J. 22
Hurford, W. 55

Inner London Education Authority (ILEA) 13, 22
Institute of Manpower Studies (IMS) 78

Jackson, K.F. 8
Jinks, D. 27, 28, 98, 99
Johnsey, R. 15, 23, 24, 25
Johnson, D.W. 52, 53
Johnson-Laird, P.N. 62
Jones, G. 55

Khaney, H. 8, 11, 14, 39, 46, 77, 133
Kelly, G.A. 62, 138
Kruger, C.J. 55
Kutnik, P. 68

Larkin, J.H. 131, 135
Levidow, L. 115
Lovejoy, S. 29

McKeachie, W.J. 74
Mahoney, M.J. 61
Mathews, B. 16, 115, 135
Michell, M. 42
Millband, C. 22
Miller, A. 81
Miller, R. 47
Minstrell, J. 60
Mitchell, I.J. 76
Munson, P. 8, 19, 102
Murphy, P. 39

National Curriculum Council (NCC) 17, 18, 19, 49, 50, 61, 64, 96

Newell, A. 131
Northern Examining Association (NEA) 118
Nott, M. 115
Novack, J. 76
Novick, S. 60
Nussbaum, J. 60

Osborne, R. 54, 64

Page, R. 29
Peacock, A. 22
Pfundt, H. 54
Poole, J. 29
Pope, M.L. 17, 62
Posner, G.J. 76, 92

Reif, F. 132
Rowlands, D. 23, 35, 39, 68

Sagan, C. 31
Saloman, G. 76
Science and Technology in Society (SATIS) 22
Screen, P. 22
Secondary Science Curriculum Review (SSCR) 22, 54, 126, 128
Shapiro, B.L. 92
Sharan, S. 68
Shayer, M. 54, 76
Shipstone, D. 55
Simon, D.P.T. 131, 135, 136
Simon, H.A. 131, 135, 136
Slack, D. 22
Slavin, R.T. 67
Solomon, J. 55
Sparkes, D. 22
Soper, R. 22
Stewart, D. 7
Strike, K.A. 76, 92
Summers, M. 55
Surrey SATRO 70, 109

Terry, C. 55
Thomas, M. 18

Urwin, C. 65

Venn, C. 65
Viennot, L. 132

Walkerdine, V. 65
Wallwork, D. 95
Watts, D.M. 4, 8, 9, 16, 17, 33, 42,
    56, 57, 58, 59, 60, 62, 66, 68, 71,
    91, 102, 115, 125, 127, 128, 131,
    132, 134
Wells, P. 55

West, A. 102, 128
White, R.T. 83
White, S. 54
Williams, H. 4
Williams, P. 27, 28, 98, 99
Woolnough, B.E. 129–30

Subject Index

Adults Other than Teachers (AOTs)
 90, 91, 99, 106
Alternative frameworks 54, 55, 58,
 135
Analogy 38, 46, 80, 128
Assessment 117-23
 self 121
 group 123
Attitudes 42, 49, 74

Biology 22, 45, 102
Brainstorming 33, 48, 60
British Association (BA) 84

Certificate of Pre-Vocational
 Education (CPVE) 113, 128,
 134-5
Chemistry 6, 44, 45, 89, 102, 131
Children's Learning in Science (CLIS)
 54, 60
Communication 15, 41, 66, 74, 96
Competition 51, 52
Conceptual change 58, 60
Constructivism 5, 17, 61-6, 74, 138
Craft, design and technology (CDT)
 20, 21, 23, 29, 98, 102, 104, 107,
 112, 113, 128
Creativity 15, 18, 27, 34, 41, 82
CREativity in Science and Technology
 (CREST) 84-91, 97, 103, 114,
 118, 119, 120, 124
Cross-curricular activities 15, 46, 88,
 98

Decision-making 8, 15, 18, 42
Dyadic pairings 68-70

English 23, 104
Equal opportunities 114-16
Experimentation 18, 42, 93
 thought experiments 6
Experts 38, 135, 136

General Certificate of Secondary
 Education (GCSE) 17, 22, 114,
 118, 119, 130, 132
GIVEN problems 8, 10, 11, 12, 19,
 32, 82, 88, 115, 131, 132
GOAL problems 8, 11, 12, 19, 32, 82
Graphicacy 34, 42
Group work 16, 42, 51, 66-72, 123

Health education 23
Heuristic search 39, 46
History 23, 102, 113
Home economics 21, 23, 108

In-service education and training
 (INSET) 124-5
Information technology (IT) 23

Knowledge
 prior 60, 63
 transfer 5

Learning
 active 4, 15, 63, 91-4, 95
 child-centred 61, 128

co-operative 52, 53, 66–72, 96
discovery 7, 15
ownership of 4, 15, 82–94, 96
transfer of 7, 14, 72, 73, 74, 75–80,
    133

Materials 100, 106, 110
Mathematics 6, 8, 16, 98, 104, 128,
    129, 131, 138
Metacognition 75
Metaphors 49, 80
Motivation 16, 67, 75, 83, 95, 127
Multicultural 68, 96, 115–16

National Curriculum
    attainment targets 17, 18, 121
    guidance 18, 50, 61
    key stages 45
    programmes of study 17
    science 2, 19, 42, 60, 132
    technology 19, 49
Novice 132, 135, 136

OWN problems 8, 10, 11, 19, 32, 37,
    82, 83, 85, 116

Physics 3, 6, 57, 58, 83, 102, 131, 138
Problem types
    closed 7, 8
    curriculum-dedicated 8, 19
    egg-race 53, 71, 97, 104, 105, 107,
        109, 111, 119, 131
    formal 8
    ill-defined 11, 12
    informal 8
    large-scale 6
    open-ended 7, 8, 10
    PS1 8, 131–2, 135, 136
    PS2 8, 131–2, 136
    technological 8, 20
    well-defined 11, 12

Problem-solving method 26, 27, 36,
    37
Problem space 32, 33, 46, 48
Project for Enhancing Effective
    Learning (PEEL) 76
Psychology 29, 113

Research 27, 35, 36, 37, 54, 74,
    125–138
Resources 39, 45, 99, 104

Schools Examination and Assessment
    Council (SEAC) 117
Science and Technology Regional
    Organizations (SATRO) 70, 84,
    124
Secondary Science Curriculum Review
    (SSCR) 22, 54, 126
Skills 4, 12–15, 20, 23, 26, 37, 40–5,
    47, 49, 61, 73, 74, 79, 118, 127,
    137
    basic 13
    core 13
    generic 13
    group 6, 72
    process 13
Standing Committee for School
    Science and Technology
    (SCSST) 8, 84
Space 10
'Structured serendipity' 36, 38, 43

Technical and Vocational Initiative
    (TVEI) 112
Technology 22, 23, 36, 101, 102
Time 37, 101

World Wide Fund for Nature (WWF)
    114, 124